VENTRILOQUISM MADE EASY

HOW TO TALK TO YOUR HAND WITHOUT LOOKING STUPID!

REVISED SECOND EDITION

By Paul Stadelman and Bruce Fife

Piccadilly Books, Ltd.
Colorado Springs, Colorado

Acknowledgments:
Pictures on pages 14, 16, 22, 23, 24, 47, and the front cover were
supplied by Stephen Axtell of Axtell Expressions. Pictures on pages
12, 13, 19, 36, 40, and 44 were supplied by Clinton Detweiler of
Maher Studios. Pictures on pages 54 and 58 were supplied by Gerry
Sparks of MasterCraft Puppets. Photo of Steve Axtell and Dazzle
Duck on front cover by Mike Gazzaway.

Copyright © 2003, 1989 by Bruce Fife
Revised Second Edition

Piccadilly Books, Ltd.
P.O. Box 25203
Colorado Springs, CO 80936, USA
info@piccadillybooks.com
www.piccadillybooks.com

Library of Congress Cataloging-in-Publication Data

Stadelman, Paul
    Ventriloquism made easy : how to talk to your hand without
looking
stupid / by Paul Stadelman.
        p.   cm.
    ISBN-13: 978-0-941599-06-1
    ISBN-10: 0-941599-06-X
    1. Ventriloquism. I. Title.
GV1557.S7 1988
793.8--dc19   88-13439

Printed in the USA

CONTENTS

Chapter 1

THE MAGIC OF VENTRILOQUISM

A WORLD OF MAKE-BELIEVE

Don't move or I'll blow your face off!" sneered the hooded figure.

Wait! You don't want to shoot me" the young detective trembled.

No? And why not?"

Because . . . ah . . . because there's a man with a gun standing behind you."

Do you think I'm STUPID? I wouldn't fall for that old—"

Drop your gun, scab, or I'll shoot!" came a voice from the back of the room.

The criminal froze and slowly let the gun drop to the floor. The youthful detective snatched up the gun and aimed it at the crook. "Now turn around and march."

As the criminal turned, his eyes searched the room. "Why, there's nobody else here!"

The detective smiled smartly, "That's right, stupid. I used ventriloquism to fool you."

Thus another villain's evil deeds were foiled by the hero's timely use of ventriloquism.

With the aid of this book, you too, can learn ventriloquism and become a hero. But rather than fight crime, you can use it to fight frowning faces and boredom. You will create laughter, and have a gaseroo of a time!

Ventriloquism is fun. What other activity will allow you to say anything to anybody with complete immunity? Imagine the things you

could say without letting anyone know it was you! You can drive your boss mad, your teachers crazy, and your girl friend wild.

In this book you will learn the "secrets" that professional ventriloquists use. You will be taught how to throw your voice and how to talk through your nose. Yes, you read that right — *talk through your nose!*

Ventriloquism offers several unique benefits. Many people who have learned ventriloquism find that it provides an enjoyable way to make extra cash in their spare time. Others find it to be a rewarding and profitable full time profession. And still others find it to be totally worthless, although entertaining. Clowns, magicians, and other family entertainers are turning to ventriloquism as a novel way to add variety to their acts. Any way you look at it, ventriloquism is a fun and a rewarding activity.

Ventriloquism is enjoyable not only because it can be used for creating comedy but because it is mysterious. Have you ever seen a professional ventriloquist and marveled at how real the figure seems to be? We forget that it's only a doll, and enter into a enchanted world where stuffed animals and puppets become real.

Magician Harry Blackstone once said, "Magicians are actors playing the part of magicians." Ventriloquists, on the other hand, are magicians playing the part of two or more actors. The ability to turn a lifeless doll into a living creature is truly magic.

The traditional image of a ventriloquist's act is that of a performer manipulating a boyish wooden doll. In my opinion it seems a little strange for a grown man to be playing with a doll. But the classic "dummy" made popular by Edgar Bergen and his partner Charlie McCarthy is that of a cheeky, smart aleck boy, and many ventriloquists still use this type of figure. Personally, I'd rather use a stuffed turkey or a gorilla. Except last time I used the turkey I had onions for lunch and his breath was terrible. Come to think of it, the gorilla wasn't any better — he stuck a banana up my nose and I couldn't talk straight.

Ventriloquism can be used not only to bring traditional ventriloquial figures and hand puppets to life, but also unconventional objects such as paper bags, gloves, and even socks. You are limited only by

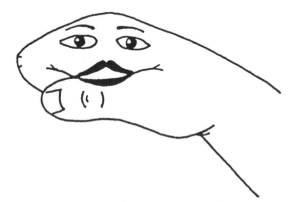

your imagination. And if your imagination is as bizarre as mine, there's no telling what you may dream up.

You don't even need props. You can use your bare hand. Draw on a pair of eyes, add nostrils and perhaps a pair of lips, and "presto" your hand has magically transformed into a talking "thing" or mini-person. It's more fun than a pocket full of toads.

Ventriloquism is exciting and can provide satisfying entertainment. Why spend a lonely night by yourself watching TV when you can slip a sock over your fist and have a delightful conversation? The two of you can go out to dinner or dancing. If anyone looks at you strangely and asks, "What are you doing?" let your sock answer with a question.

Most likely the person will answer back to your sock. You then look at him queerly and say, "Why are you talking to my gym socks?"

You don't have to be crazy to be a ventriloquist—but it helps.

VENTRILOQUISM THE EASY WAY

Most people are surprised when I tell them that ventriloquism is not throwing the voice or talking with immovable lips. Oh sure, that's part of it, but ventriloquism is much more. The art of ventriloquism is the ability or skill of bringing inanimate objects to life. A voice alone will not convince an audience that a puppet or ventriloquial figure is a living creature. The voice must sound convincing, be distinctively different from your natural voice, show emotion, and be synchro-nized with the puppet's lips and body movements. The combination of these skills makes up the art of ventriloquism.

If you're reading this book to learn some "tricks" for throwing your voice and speaking without lip movement, I won't disappoint you. I'll reveal the tricks used to master the art of imperceptible speech, to throw your voice, and talk through your nose. Even though I will show you how to accomplish these things, the real secret to ventriloquism is *practice*. I will show you what to do, but if you don't take the time to practice, it will be of little use.

Don't let the need to practice scare you. When I first started to learn ventriloquism I could hardly even say the word, let alone do

Paul Stadelman, Windy Higgins, and Fehr's Bear. Both Windy and the Bear are hard bodied figures. The bear is made of a light plastic covered with synthetic fur and is operated with a rod and lever like other "hard" figures.

it! Yet now, after many years of practice, I can say it pretty well. Ventriloquism is fun, and the basics can be learned in a relatively short time. In this book I present ventriloquism in a way that is easy to understand and learn. That's why I came up with the clever and highly original title of *Ventriloquism Made Easy.*

Like most professional ventriloquists, I'm self taught, but it's a little known fact that I learned ventriloquism in only two weeks. That's right, two weeks. This is the way it happened. I was playing a return date as a magician when the man who booked the act came up to me and asked if I could do a "vent" act. I'd never done one before, but at that time I was always eager for work, so I said, "Sure!" And he booked me for two spots on the show. I immediately wired a dealer for a vent figure, and while waiting for it, I started to write material and practice lip and voice control.

Back in those days, ventriloquists were scarce, and although I had worked on the same bill with several, I had never handled a figure. I had a fair idea of how to use the voice, but I really wasn't sure. To make a long story short, the manager was so enthused with my new act that he said I should "junk the magic and stick to vent." I never did tell him that he was paying for my debut as a ventriloquist. I learned a lot of things in those two weeks. It has taken me several years to unlearn some of the mistakes, but I'll start you off in the right direction.

If I could learn ventriloquism well enough to start performing after only two weeks, so can you. In fact, you have an advantage over me. I didn't have a book like this to help me out.

In this book I'll show you how to develop a ventriloquial voice and how to use it effectively with your puppet partner. The techniques I use are simple and have been used successfully by puppeteers and ventriloquists for many years. Although other methods exist, I'll show you techniques that are easy to learn.

Do these methods work? I use them myself and have had great success. Many of the top ventriloquists working today use them. So yes, they do work, and I promise you that any person of average intelligence who has normal vocal cords and enough ambition to practice can become a successful ventriloquist.

Chapter 2

VENTRILOQUIAL PUPPETRY

PUPPETS AND VENTRILOQUIAL FIGURES

While you read this book you should have a puppet or ventriloquial figure to practice with. Don't get a cheap practice figure. Buy a good figure, whose expression and color appeal to you, and make up your mind that you will keep it, dress it in good clothes, and take care of it. It will be expensive, but it will be worth it.

Ventriloquial dolls and hand puppets of all varieties can be obtained at your local magic shop or ordered through the mail. Several reputable mail order dealers are listed in the appendix of this book. If you can't find anything locally, write to them for a catalog.

I've seen some cheap plastic vent figures sold in local chain stores with a price tag of under $15. The mouth is operated by pulling a string, which is difficult to control, and the head is all but immovable. These figures are toys, unsuitable for our purpose. Although not impossible to use, it would take some creative innovation to make such a figure lifelike. So please avoid the idea of getting a cheap practice figure and get something you can really work with.

There are basically two types of vent figures: soft and hard. The hard figures are made of wood, plastic, or fiberglass. The head is mounted on a rod which extends down into the chest cavity. Turning the rod moves the figure's head. A lever on the rod operates the mouth. Top quality wooden figures may run up to as much as $1500 or more. This may be too expensive for you right now, but you can get good wooden and plastic figures for well under $200.

Hard ventriloquial figures, or dummies as they are frequently called, are made of wood, fiberglass, or plastic. The ventriloquist operates the mouth and head by a rod and control lever in the figure's chest cavity.

Soft human and animal ventriloquial puppets.

Soft figures are made of cloth, rubber, and other materials and usually fit over the hand. The mouth, head, and body are manipulated by the ventriloquist's hand and wrist. Decent inexpensive cloth figures can be purchased for as little as $30. Some custom-made puppets, however, can cost several hundred dollars.

NOVELTY FIGURES

Traditionally ventriloquists have used the smart aleck little boy figure, with the puppet as the comic and the vent as the straight man.

Nowadays there is an increasing trend toward originality. Wood and plastic boy figures are still the most popular, but animal figures and soft Bert and Ernie-type figures are gaining great popularity, especially with young audiences. Figures which are now being used include old men, girls, grandmothers, space creatures, bugs, dogs, cats, parrots, monkeys, rabbits, spiders, snakes, and frogs, to name just a few.

Novelty hand puppets come in a variety of styles ranging from Ronald Reagan look-alikes to alligators and ducks. The figures shown here are made with flexible rubber heads which allow the ventriloquist to operate the mouth. Exaggerated facial expressions can be created by the way the ventriloquist holds and squeezes the face.

Figures don't need to be restricted to animals and humans, but can include almost any object where the ventriloquist can create the illusion of intelligence. Senor Wences made his hand famous by adding a couple of eyes and forming moving lips with his thumb and first finger. Other unique figures include: pictures and statues with moving mouths, beer mugs, walking sticks, skulls, hats, books, scarves, and gloves. Some creative performers have even trained live dogs to open their mouths while they speak in a gruff voice. Just about anything is possible. Let's take a closer look at a few novelty figures.

The Sock Puppet
Sheri Lewis made the sock puppet popular with her companions Lambchop and Charlie Horse. A variety of puppets can be created by using various types of socks.

For illustrative purposes take a gym sock (or any sock hanging around, preferably a clean one) and put your hand inside as pictured here.

Tucking the end of the sock between the fingers and thumb forms the puppet's mouth. You may want to put a rubber band over the knuckles of the top four fingers to keep the sock in place.

With a felt-tip marker you can lightly mark where to place the lips, nose, eyes, and ears. Using cloth, felt, or buttons these features can be sewn on. Craft stores carry plastic eyes, noses, and other items that can be used to make the face. Yarn or fake fur can be used for the hair. If you want to keep the cost of your first practice figure down, the sock puppet is the cheapest way to go.

Just to get the feel of the sock puppet, grab a sock and put it on your hand. With the sock in place you can display a variety of emotions by manipulating the thumb and fingers. Raising your first and little fingers above the two middle fingers produces a smile. Lowering the two outer fingers below the thumb makes the puppet frown. Curling the thumb and fingers back puckers its lips to make it show displeasure. You can make it appear to be sticking out its tongue by curling the fingers back while keeping the thumb out straight. Thinking, as to say "hmm," is shown by sliding the thumb to one side and lowering the pinky slightly. To make the puppet spit or say "pewy," curl all the fingers and quickly straighten them out as you open the puppet's mouth.

If your puppet gets angry, you can form a fist and "sock" yourself. In the same vein it can slap, point, and shake hands, turning briefly into a gloved hand to accomplish a desired affect and then changing quickly back into a puppet. You can get a lot of humor out of this sort of thing.

With a little imagination, a sock puppet can be a lot of fun. I've used sock puppets for small groups of kids and had a blast. Children get so excited that they can't wait to grab a sock of their own and try it out. You may find them sitting around taking off their shoes to do just that.

Third Arm Puppetry

The ventriloquist walks out on stage. Perched on his arm is a large bird. Both of the ventriloquist's arms and hands are free and plainly visible, yet the bird is totally animated. It turns its head and neck in almost any direction and moves its lips when speaking. Unlike most vent figures it can be viewed from all sides without revealing the secret, creating the perfect illusion.

How is it done? Simple. The vent uses a fake third arm which looks like his own. The bird, which rests on his elbow, is manipulated

by the ventriloquist's hand and forearm. His real arm fits through an opening in the coat sleeve to operate the puppet.

There are other ways of using third arm puppetry. If you cut a hole in your coat above the breast pocket, your arm can fit through. A box can be held against your chest, concealing the hole. Your fake arm wraps around the box as if holding it. Your hidden arm is then free to manipulate a puppet (your pet dog, cat, bird, or whatever) who happens to be inside the box. The puppet can pop out of the box to torment you.

For variation, instead of a box you could use a sack, suitcase, talking potted plant, or stack of books with a talkative bookworm who keeps popping out of the cover of the top book.

Another way to present the third arm illusion is to hold a container with a fake hand. A top hat, for example, can be held and a mischievous rabbit pop up to help the ventriloquist (or clown or magician) who is trying to perform magic. This idea has a lot of potential for effective humor.

Living Figures

For a novel twist, instead of using a lifeless figure that you make look alive, use a living figure and make him or her look like a dummy. Have a volunteer (child or adult) come up and be the dummy.

Explain to the volunteer that when you squeeze (gently) on his neck he is to open his mouth. When you relax your grip, he is to close his mouth. If you do this with children you should simplify the instructions and have the volunteer merely open and close his mouth with each squeeze.

With your hand on the back of your volunteer's neck you can turn his head so that he can look wherever you want him to.

When you begin to talk to your "living dummy," at first he will be unsure of what's happening and his lips may not be in synchronization with your vent voice, or he may actually speak to answer a question, making the routine even funnier. You may even purposely get his lips out of synchronization or pretend to ask him a question to lead him into these types of situations.

For added comic effect, use a high pitched voice if an adult is helping you, and use a deep voice for a child.

This type of presentation can be a scream, especially if all of the members of the audience know each other, such as at birthday parties. If you use the guest of honor or a popular member of the audience as the dummy, everyone will love it.

The Talking Tie

Your partner doesn't need to be a human, an animal, or an insect. It can be an inanimate object brought to life by the magic of ventriloquism.

A relatively new gimmick on the market is the talking tie, sold by Maher Studios. This clip-on tie comes with movable eyes and mouth, which is operated by pulling a hidden string. The mouth remains nearly unseen until the string is pulled to open it up.

Imagine the look on people's faces as they glance at an innocent looking tie with eyes and see it move and talk.

A brief dialogue might go something like this:

Tie: Hello.
Ventriloquist: Who said that?
T: Me.
V: Me who?
T: What do you think you are a cat?
V: Where are you?
T: I'm down here.
V: I don't see anybody.
T: Look at your stomach.
V: Now don't get personal.
T: I'm just telling you where I am.
V: Oh no, my stomach is talking to me. It must have been the

*Novelty figures as shown here range in style from a talkative tie to
a blabbering banana.*

spicy fig balls I had for lunch.

T: I'm not your stomach, you idiot. I'm your tie.

V: That's impossible. I don't believe it.

T: You mean to say a talking tie is impossible but a talking tummy isn't?

V: Well er . . . ah . . . gosh. You really are talking. I've got a talking tie! What are you doing here?

T: Oh, nothing much. Just hanging around.

V: No, I mean where did you come from?

T: Why Tie-wan, of course.

V: But how did you learn to talk?

T: I took a speech class.

V: Where?

T: (Loudly) YALE!

V: I think you should have gone to that Italian school.

T: What one is that?

V: Shut Upa U.

Balloon Figures

Magicians, clowns, and other family entertainers often give away balloons twisted into cute little animal shapes. At birthday parties, picnics, and other gatherings these colorful figures make ideal gifts. They are inexpensive and easy to make, but most of all, *kids love them!* Inflate a skinny little balloon and create an animal, and watch a child's face light up with excitement. Even adults have a hard time controlling themselves.

Why should magicians and clowns have all the fun? Ventriloquists can join in the excitement of balloon sculpturing and make talking balloon animals. In the book *Dewey's Balloon and Clown Notebook* Ralph Dewey describes how to make a cute, bubbly rabbit with a movable mouth from a single pencil balloon. But a movable mouth isn't required in order to have fun with talking balloon figures. The illusion of talking can still be created if both of you look at each other while in conversation and if you move the figure up and down slightly as it talks.

Before the eyes of the audience you can create a balloon animal, bring it to life, and carry on a conversation. When the routine
is over, the balloon can be given to someone in the audience. If it's
a small crowd you can make balloon figures for everyone. That way
the kids receive more than just a balloon to take home, they receive
part of the show! You've given the balloon figure a name and a
personality, making it real. The kids will get a kick out of copying you
and making their own animals "talk."

Radios and Other Electrical Gadgets

Radios make easy props for vent acts. People are accustomed
to listening to radios so a talking portable radio is not beyond belief.

Since the radio doesn't have a moving mouth to help create the
illusion of talking, a small light must be added. Each time the radio
speaks the light will flash on and off. The light being operated by a
switch on the back. When the light flashes and the audience hears

Three cartoon-like hand puppets (shown left to right) a parrot, cockatoo, and dodo.

the voice it will appear as if the radio were talking. You can be listening to the radio and disagree or make a comment on something the disc jockey says which would lead into an argument. Or start singing along with a song and have the person in the radio tell you to shut up.

This idea also can be used with other electrical devices such as telephones, televisions, mini robots, and personal computers.

As you're walking past a phone booth, the phone begins to ring. Stop, pick it up, and have a conversation with a lonely phone. Or, the person on the other end of the line may have dialed the wrong number. The caller may think he has phoned home to his wife and wants to know why you are there.

A television would be similar to the radio. The picture tube could flash brightly each time it speaks. Another way to use it would be to manipulate hand or finger puppets inside the set. You would then hold a conversation with the actors on the screen.

Robots and computers have not yet been used very frequently by ventriloquists, but they too can be adapted easily to this sort of act. Both are often depicted as having minds of their own, so creating the illusion of life would not be difficult.

The Magic Drawing Board

The Magic Drawing Board, which is manufactured and sold by Axtell Expressions, is one of the most creative props I've seen on the market. It consists of a blank drawing board with a light blue grid covered with plastic. Pictures can be drawn on the board with an ordinary marker and then erased with a cloth.

The unique part about this board is that while a face is being drawn, the eyes and the mouth can move. Right before everyone's eyes the picture comes to life and starts to talk. The eyes move from side to side and the mouth opens and closes, all under the artist's complete control. After talking with the animated drawing it can be completely erased—even while it's moving! A mind boggling effect.

Any type of picture can be drawn and made to come to life. It could be people faces, animals, or whatever. When introduced for the

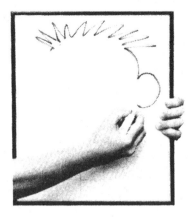 

first time several years ago at the International Ventriloquists ConVENTion, the Magic Drawing Board was an immediate hit. Since then it has been used successfully by magicians and clowns as well as ventriloquists.

Chapter 3

THE ART OF
IMPERCEPTIBLE SPEECH

TEACHING YOUR PARTNER TO TALK

I believe that you will learn faster if you start your first lesson on voice while actually operating the figure. Approach your study of ventriloquism with the idea that you are going to bring your puppet to life. Don't think of it as a doll, but as your partner or co-star and teach it how to talk.

If you have the imagination to approach the study of ventriloquism from that angle instead of thinking of yourself as learning to be a ventriloquist, you will not only learn faster but you will enjoy every minute you practice.

I also recommend that, if possible, you take your book and your partner into a private room for your practice session. You will learn faster if no one sees you in the progressive stage. You are not yet ready to perform. And besides, to people who don't know what you're doing, it looks a little odd to be talking to your hand or to a doll.

To start, sit down facing a large mirror and put the figure on your lap. With your natural voice, and without trying to use ventriloquism, have the figure say, "Hello, how are you?" Remember, you're teaching your partner to talk, so open and close the figure's mouth as you pronounce each syllable. Try it.

Not much illusion, is there? Now, with your lips slightly parted, but without moving them, repeat the action.

Still not too good? With the same action, lips immovable, and tongue tip curled back slightly behind your upper teeth, try it again.

Not bad, eh? Now, same action, immovable lips, tongue tip curled back as before, lungs full of air, and expelled as you speak, try it again.

Say, that time he really talked, didn't he?

When you're speaking for the figure the proper position of the mouth should be with lips and teeth slightly parted and the entire face relaxed. Do not form the habit of clenching the teeth, as this cuts down the volume of the voice and slightly muffles the tone.

With your mouth and tongue in this position, try saying the following sentences without moving your lips:

Catch that ghost.
Nothing succeeds like success.
It's a teenie weenie sausage.
There's a hole in his head.
She sells sea shells at the sea shore.

That was pretty good, wasn't it? Hardly any lip movement. How did your partner do? Was the movement of his lips synchronized so that they opened and closed with each syllable? Go back and practice the sentences one more time before continuing.

Don't be fooled by the simplicity of these sentences. You're off to a good start, but you still have a long way to go.

HOW TO SPEAK THROUGH YOUR NOSE

Speaking through the nose? Yes, that's right. Does it sound amazing? . . . Yes . . . Does it sound gross? . . . No, not any more than your normal speech is. Is it hard? . . . No. In fact, you do it all the time without even realizing it. The ability to force your words up through the nose is one of the secrets of ventriloquism and mastering the art of imperceptible speech.

In normal speech your lips and tongue combine to pronounce words. In ventriloquism you must train the tongue to take over the lips' job so your mouth can appear motionless.

Skeptical? . . . Here's a little exercise you can do to illustrate the fact that you do indeed use your nose in speech. Say the letter "m." Notice that as you pronounce this letter *your lips are closed.*

Say it again, but this time hold the sound as if humming: "mmmm." Where is the sound coming from? It's not coming out of your mouth because you have that closed. You made the sound come out of your nose! If you don't believe me, try humming while holding your nose. You can't do it unless you open your mouth to release the sound. By the way, make sure no one sees you while you're doing this; it could be embarrassing.

You don't need to close your lips in order to channel sound through your nose. The tongue can block the passage of air, redirecting your voice through the nose. When you say the letter "n," for example, notice that your tongue is pushed up against the roof of your mouth.

The voice comes up from your vocal cords in your throat and is blocked by the tongue and redirected up through the nose. So you see, talking through your nose is no big deal. You've done it all your life.

Now that I've convinced you that speaking through the nose is possible you are ready to learn about the labial consonants.

LABIAL CONSONANTS

A baby's first distinguishable word is usually "daddy." It's much later that he says "mama." Your partner will have the same trouble because "daddy" is articulated by touching the tongue twice to the upper front of the mouth while expelling the breath, while in saying "mama" each "m" is formed by bringing the lips together.

Try to say "mama" without moving your lips.

Can't do it? Some words are harder than others. I will now show you how to handle hard to pronounce words.

The practice sentences at the beginning of this chapter were easy. Look in a mirror and try the following sentences, keeping your lips absolutely motionless:

A lazy daisy sleeps in the field.
Ventriloquism is for dummies.
A hobo in the rain is a damp tramp.
Do fish close their eyes when they sleep?
Ring around the rosy, fall down and break your nosey.
No matter how young a prune may be, it's always full of
    wrinkles.
Baby bumblebees don't bite.

Not too successful were you? Unlike the sentences you tried earlier, these contain what are known as labial consonants. To pronounce words containing labial consonants, lip movement is normally needed.

Go back to the mirror. Speaking as you normally would, slowly recite the alphabet. Watch your lips as you say each letter. Do it now.

Many of the letters you just recited needed little or no lip movement while others used a lot. Part your teeth and lips slightly, keeping your face relaxed, and try the alphabet again with as little lip movement as possible.

You will notice that most of the letters can be pronounced without much noticeable lip movement. Several of the letters which require movement in normal speech, such as **A**, **C**, **D**, **G**, **O**, and **U**, can be pronounced with the aid of the tongue, without using the lips.

As you recited the alphabet there were a few letters — **F**, **V**, **P**, **B**, **M**, and **W** — that needed lip movement for clear pronunciation. In fact, they seem to be impossible to say without moving the lips. These six letters are the labial consonants.

When saying the letters **P**, **B**, **M**, and **W**, you will notice your lips coming together slightly. The other two labials, **F** and **V**, are pronounced by touching the lower lip lightly to the upper teeth. When pronouncing these letters normally you must move the lips for proper articulation.

TRICKS OF THE TRADE

If it weren't for the labials, a ventriloquist's job would be easy. It is important that you learn how to handle these letters if you want to become a good ventriloquist, or even just a mediocre one. Let's discuss some of the "tricks of the trade" for getting around labials.

Deletion

The simplest method for handling labials is to simply dodge them. Choose words for your dialogue that do not contain labials. If the dialogue has a word with a labial, replace the word with a synonym or with another word that has a similar meaning. For example, instead of using the word "leopard," use "lion" or "tiger." Instead of "boot" say "shoe." Get the idea?

The following sentences contain words with labials. Each sentence is paired with a possible alternative which will allow you to avoid lip movement. In some cases you may need to change the entire sentence to find suitable wording.

Did you ever see a crocodile *smile*?
Did you ever see a crocodile grin?

As clear as *mud*.
As clear as night.

A *fly* walked into the grocery store.
An ant walked into the grocery store.

Please give *me* a glass of water.
Could I have a glass of water?

Completely avoiding words with labials can be difficult and although short conversations can be worked up, longer dialogues would take a great deal of effort to construct. Therefore it is best to learn to pronounce words containing labials. To do this you will need to learn the substitution method.

Substitution

You can approximate the sounds of the labial consonants by using other letters in their place. The techniques for doing this are known as the *substitution method* or *false speech*.

It will take a little practice to become familiar with each of the substitutions, but it's like learning to ride a bicycle; after a while it will feel natural and you'll do it automatically.

Sit in front of a mirror in a comfortable position. Without moving your lips, say this sentence: "Where are you going, Frank?"

You'll find it easy to say all of the words in this sentence without moving your lips except for the word "Frank." On the **F** you will notice your bottom lip coming up to touch your upper teeth.

The sound which can best be substituted for **F** is **TH** as in the word "throw." The word "throw" can be pronounced without lip movement. Practice the following words replacing the **F** with **TH**:

face = thace	fact = thact
fall = thall	few = thew
field = thield	find = thind
fish = thish	flag = tlag
flame = thlame	follow = thollow
forest = thorest	fossil = thossil
front = thront	fruit = thruit
future = thuture	fuzz = thuzz

At first this substitution may not sound too accurate to you. If you think **F** as you make the substitution you will progress faster. As you practice, your pronunciation will improve and your substitution will be undetectable. Practice the following dialogue, substituting **TH** for **F** when the figure is speaking:

V: What did you take to school for your teacher?
P: A *flower*.
V: Did she like it?
P: No, one of my *friends* ate it.
V: How did that happen?
P: I stuck it inside his tuna *fish* sandwich.

Say, you did pretty well! It almost sounded as if you were really pronouncing the **F**. When used in a sentence, substitutions for labials become less detectable.

Now let's work on our next labial, the letter **V**. The substitute for **V** is very similar to the used for **F**. You will use **TH** but make it a little softer as in the word "THERE." Try the following words replacing the softer **TH** for **V**.

vanity = thanity	vacancy = thacancy
vague = thague	value = thalue
vault = thault	very = thery
victory = thictory	visible = thisible
visitor = thisitor	vine = thine

Practice this list of words a few of more times before continuing on.

Now let's try some of these words in sentences.

Put the money in the *vault*.
The score was *very* close.
He is a *visitor*.
The *victory* was ours.

Most of the words we have practiced so far use a substitution on the first letter, but when **F** or **V** come in the middle of the word, such as "safety" or "curve," the same substitution applies.

Some ventriloquists find it easier to pronounce the **F** and **V** using a still lip. To use this method relax your face and separate your lips and teeth. Gently touch your lower lip to your upper teeth. You can do this easily in a natural looking manner. With your mouth in this position you will find that you can pronounce all of the non-labials as well as **F** and **V** without lip movement.

We will now take a look at the letter **W**. This is the easiest labial to use in speech. By itself it is pronounced as "double-you," which contains another labial, **B** (which we will cover later). When used in a word **W** is pronounced more like **OO**, as in "boo." This **OO** sound is easily pronounced without the aid of the lips. Try these words:

        when = oohen
        why = oohy
        where = oohere
        wind = ooind
        water = ooater

That wasn't hard, was it? Another break we get is that in many words the **W** is silent, such as in "whole," "write," and "wrong". It's time for a practice sentence.

Walter Whipple whistles while wading in the water for a wrinkled white whale.

By this time you should be at the point where you and your partner can carry on short conversations. As you watch the two of you in the mirror, the illusion should be growing that he is talking. Of course his pronunciation isn't perfect. There are some words he can't say at all, for instance, "rubber buggy bumpers," but who wants to go around saying "rubber buggy bumpers" all the time?

The remaining three labials **M**, **P**, and **B** are a bit more difficult to master and will take a little more practice. But if you follow my directions you will be talking like a true ventriloquist before you know it.

Each of these three letters can be handled by substituting easier letters. Let's start with the letter **M**.

The simpelest substitution for **M** is a modified **N**. For example, "marry" becomes "narry," "money" becomes "noney."

Making these substitutions produces similar sounding words that may slip past some listeners, but to make the substitution convincing to everyone you will need to modify the way you say **N**. Say "**N**" out loud. Did you notice that as you said it the tip of your tongue touched the roof of your mouth? Say it again. You will modify the position of the tongue slightly when making your substitution. Instead of letting your tongue touch the roof of your mouth, push your tongue lightly against the back of the upper front teeth. Say "**N**" but think "**M**."

Practice the following words, using the **N** substitute:

mad = nad	make = nake
march = narch	margin = nargin
marriage = narriage	master = naster
melody = nelody	menu = nenu
mild = nild	milk = nilk
miracle = niracle	mirror = nirror
modern = nodern	morning = norning
most = nost	more = nore
music = nusic	mystery = nystery

How was your pronunciation? Did these words sound like they had an **M** in them? Practice this list of words one more time.

Now try the following sentence.

Mary's mother makes money making mincemeat pies on Monday.

The next letter we'll tackle is **P**. It is handled in a similar way **M** was. The substitution you will use is a modified **T**. Say "**T**" in your normal voice. Did you notice that when you did this, the tip of your tongue touched the roof of your mouth? When you say "**T**" to make the **P** substitution, press the top of your tongue against the roof of your mouth and touch the tip of your tongue to the back of your upper front teeth. Say "**T**" with your tongue in this position. When making the **P** substitution this is the position your tongue should be in. As you make the substitution, cut it a little short and pop the **P** sound out.

Using this substitution try your hand (or rather your tongue) at the following words:

painful = tainful	pardon = tardon
part = tart	pass = tass
play = tlay	picture = ticture
pickup = tickup	pie = tie
plug = tlug	penny = tenny
plot = tlot	point = toint
polish = tolish	pour = tour
person = terson	press = tress
print = trint	push = tush

How did you do? Did the substitution sound like a **P** or a **T**? At first you may feel that it's impossible to make the **T** sound like a **P**, and you're right. A **T** will always sound like a **T** if you think of it merely as a substitution. What's important is that you have the correct tongue position and as you say "**T**," think "**P**". If you practice with this thought in mind you will train your tongue to pronounce **P**. Go back over the list of words and practice it a couple of more times thinking "**P**".

Try this tongue twister for practice:

Peter Piper picked a peck of pickled peppers.

Hand puppets can sit in the lap like traditional ventriloquial figures (page 50), set on a stand (page 23), rest on the arm or appear to (page 17), or even float in the air (page 62). Large figures, such as the one pictured here, can appear to stand on thier own.

The last substitution you will need to know is for the letter **B**. To produce the **B** sound you will replace it with a modified **D**. This is done in a similar fashion as you did with the **P** and **T** substitution.

Notice that when you say "**D**" the tip of your tongue touches the roof of your mouth. Modify this position as you did with the **T** substitution by pressing your tongue against the top of your mouth and the back of your upper front teeth. Cut the substitution short and pop the **B** sound out.

You're ready for some practice now.

ball = dall	back = dack
balance = dalance	bald = dald
base = dase	because = decause
below = delow	belt = delt
bend = dend	big = dig
bill = dill	black = dlack
blind = dlind	blow = dlow
board = doard	brush = drush
building = duilding	business = dusiness

Did you remember to think "**B**" as you made your substitutions? Practice this list two more times before going any further.

Before we leave the **B**, practice the following sentence:

Beautiful Betty boasted better biscuits than Bonita.

We've now covered all of the substitutions you will need to know. In summary they are:

F = TH (as in throw)	M = N
V = TH (as in there)	P = T
W = OO	B = D

Notice that in all of these sounds except the **W** the tongue is pressed against the back of the upper front teeth, directing your breath up through the nose. This is the secret of pronouncing the labials ventriloquially.

As you practice if you will think of the original letter rather than of the substitution your pronunciation will become clearer. You will get closer and closer to actually saying **F, V, M, P,** and **B.** It will even sound accurate and true to you, although at no time do you actually say these letters by this method.

HELPFUL HINTS

Although your substitutions can simulate the labials a few of helpful hints will make slight variations in pronunciation less detectable.

The first hint is to put emphasis on the words without labials. For example, in the sentence "I can play the guitar," if you emphasize "guitar," slight variations in the word "play" ("tlay") will not be noticed.

Another idea to keep in mind is not to use so many labials in the figure's lines as to be noticed by your audience. For instance, if you say "oken, oken, oken" to a friend and ask him to repeat what you said, he would say, "oken, oken, oken." But if you say to him, "oken the door," he would open the door and notice nothing unusual about it. A door is thought of as either opened or closed. The same idea applies when the figure is singing a popular song. The audience is mentally repeating the words with him, so if he should sing "girl of ny dreangs" to them, it will sound like "girl of my dreams."

For small groups, such as children's birthday parties or business promotions, you will be very close to your audience and will need to refrain from moving your lips as much as possible.

When working in front of a large crowd or on a stage you will probably have a microphone and be at least ten feet away from the audience. In this type of situation you will be able to move your lips slightly without detection. The microphone amplifies the voice so that you can speak softly and your lips need not be separated so much. At a distance of 10 or 15 feet, my mouth looks as though it were closed. In this position it is easy to touch the lips together for an occasional labial, especially if you turn your head slightly toward the figure as you speak these letters.

When working with a microphone, don't place it in front of your face. About chest level is best. Never look at the mike, but always remember where it is and talk over it instead of into it.

It's a good idea to have a lot of volume on the microphone and then speak softly for both yourself and your figure. If you are using a figure with a slot-jaw be careful not to release the jaw movement so fast that the clicking is picked up by the microphone.

You're ready for one final exercise before going to the next chapter. Using everything you've learned so far about substitution, try saying the following sentences without moving your lips. Use a mirror to help you out.

A *penny* saved is a *penny* earned.
Birds of a feather *flock* together.
The early *bird* catches the *worm*.
Too *many* cooks *spoil* the *broth*.
Barking dogs never *bite*.
Easy *come*, easy go.
He who *fights* and runs away *may* live to *fight* another day.
A *friend* in need is a *friend* indeed.
Laugh and grow *fat*.
Though the *bird* may *fly* over your head, let it not *make* its nest in your hair.

Chapter 4

BRINGING YOUR PARTNER TO LIFE

CREATING CHARACTER

One of the most important ways to make your partner appear as though alive is to give it a distinct and separate personality. It is also important that this personality be consistent. The audience expects the "performers" to have separate personalities. If they don't, the audience becomes confused and the figure loses appeal, making it appear more like an object than a living creature.

What type of personality traits should your partner have? Use the following list to help define your partner's character. Is it male or female; young or old; happy or grumpy; rude or well mannered; clumsy or skilled; smart or dumb; brave or cowardly?

To help you build an interesting character, you should give your puppet preferences on subjects such as music, clothes, sports, friends, and food.

What about his education and background? Where was he born? Was it in the city or country? Did he graduate from high school, clown college, medical school, a space academy, or is he still in school?

What does he do for a profession? Is he a entertainer, singer, dancer, cowboy, farmer, cook, student, or hobo?

Use these ideas to help define your partner's character and always keep your puppet in character when you perform.

THE VENTRILOQUIAL VOICE

One of the elements of ventriloquism which makes your partner appear as a separate being is having a distinct voice, one that is clearly different from your own. You will need to experiment with different types of voices for your partner. In this section we will explore ways of discovering the right voice for your partner.

Take your partner on your lap, with your lips slightly separated and face relaxed experiment talking at different pitches. Find a pitch you feel comfortable with and practice some of the exercises from the last chapter. Practice this voice now before going any farther.

Eventually, you will get a voice that fits. In other words, that is the way your partner would sound if it could really talk. You may find the right voice in a few minutes, or it might be several days, but satisfy yourself that it is what you want, and once you get it, stick to it.

Please make this decision yourself. If you ask your friends, one will say it is too high, another too low. Satisfy yourself that your chosen voice is how you want your partner to talk. Sell yourself on the idea, because it is you who will later sell your audience.

It is not necessary to have his voice higher or lower than yours, if you can produce a voice that is absolutely different form your own, that is sufficient. Of course if you are using a figure of a very young character, and you are a deep baritone, then you should use a higher pitch, but the worst thing a vent can do is to use a squeaky high pitched voice.

When choosing a voice for your partner, you need to keep in mind that the voice must reflect the puppet's character. You must also be able to speak clearly so you can be easily understood. And you must be able to maintain a conversation without undue stress.

What type of character is your partner? Would a deep rough voice be better than a high-pitched one? Is the character a smart aleck, a grouch, a dope, silly, tough, elderly, or mechanical? The voice you choose should be consistent with your puppet's personality.

Try to define your puppet's character as much as possible with the voice you choose. A squeaky voice may be suitable for a mouse but would be out of place for a lumber jack, policeman, bear, or toad.

Clinton Detweiler, director of Maher Studios, manipulates soft buzzard ventriloquial puppet.

Watch the children's shows on TV and listen to how the characters talk. Watch cartoons, Sesame Street, and other shows. This will help give you ideas.

A careful choice of slang or descriptive words and an accent can help out tremendously in giving your puppet character. Be careful not to overdo it. You don't want to become hard to understand; audiences, especially young ones, get restless if they can't follow the conversation.

Practice teaching your puppet to talk using the vent voice. A tape recorder can be useful. Listing to yourself on the recorder can help you become aware of problems in your speech you might not otherwise notice.

Now read through the following short dialogues and practice your vent voice. Use your normal voice for one character and your puppet's voice for the other. It may seem confusing at first but practice makes perfect. The V stands for ventriloquist and the P for partner.

P: Where did you get that nice Easter tie?
V: What makes you think it's an Easter tie?
P: It's got egg on it.

V: What did you get that little silver medal for?
P: For singing.
V: What did you get that big gold medal for?
P: For stopping.

V: Did you study for your first aid test?
P: Yep.
V: OK, let me quiz you. What's the best way to prevent infection caused by biting insects?
P: That's easy, don't bite any.

V: Is the horn on your car broken?
P: No, it's just indifferent.
V: What do you mean, indifferent?
P: It just doesn't give a hoot.

V: What are you doing with that pencil and paper?
P: I'm writing a letter to my brother.
V: Who are you kidding? You know you don't know how to write.
P: Sure, but my brother doesn't know how to read, either.

ANIMATION AND MANIPULATION
Puppet Animation

Having a unique voice for your puppet and using a clever dialogue will do a great deal in making your partner "live." Hearing a voice and seeing the puppet's lips move while yours do not, will create the illusion that the puppet can speak. But even though your lips may be perfectly still, if your puppet's movements are unnatural or awkward, the illusion will be destroyed. To really make your puppet come alive, you must use animation. You must manipulate the puppet so that it mimics the movement and actions of a living creature.

The most basic movement to master is the puppet's mouth. Each syllable must be synchronized with the opening and closing of the puppet's lips. Lips which are not in harmony with the words look fake—even to the youngest viewer. By now you should already have a good deal of practice synchronizing syllables with your puppet's mouth movements.

Once you've mastered lip synchronization, you should practice using body language. Avoid holding the figure stiffly when he talks. Remember you are trying to give the illusion that the puppet is a living, intelligent creature. To create this illusion, the puppet needs to reenforce his thoughts and words with physical movement. Just as people move their arms and body while in conversation, so should your puppet. Tilt its head a little to one side or the other, give a slight turn now and then. Twist its body, lean it forward and back or from side to side, have it jump and move its head in all directions—even upside down if you need to. Have it chew on props, mess your hair, or give you a hug. When you ask it a question, let it hesitate a few seconds before answering. These actions will give your partner life and character. But don't make the mistake of jiggling the head continually; it's distracting and will make your audience nervous.

One of the most common mistakes beginners make is ignoring the puppet's eye contact. When your partner speaks to you, he should be looking at your face and not at the floor. You need to be consciously aware of where your partner is looking at all times. Would you look at someone's shoe and say "I like your hat?" If your partner says "Is it going to rain?" he should be looking towards the sky. Making your partner see is one of the most important principals in learning to manipulate a puppet properly.

Some figures, however, don't have movable mouths, so how do you make them appear to talk? You don't need the mouth to move for them to talk. Even without the figure's lips moving, you can create the illusion that the puppet is talking by careful body manipulation. Moving the puppet's head or body while giving him a voice will make it appear as though he is talking. Give him full actions. Have him

point to himself when he says "me," rub his eyes when crying, shake the head "no" and nod "yes." Have him act out as much of his dialogue as possible. You should do this even with figures which do have mouths, but it's especially important for those that do not.

Watch children in conversation if you want to learn natural movements for your partner. If he is a very young character and the pert, sassy type, watch a small boy of the type. Note the quick movements of his head, the glib answer (even though it is wrong), the quick change of subject if you pin him down on a statement he makes. If he is a little older type, then his answers are more positive, the head movements not so fast.

If he is the stupid type, facially and in character and dialogue, then his movements are much slower. You have to repeat the questions, at times, and when you ask a question, he looks at you, then at the

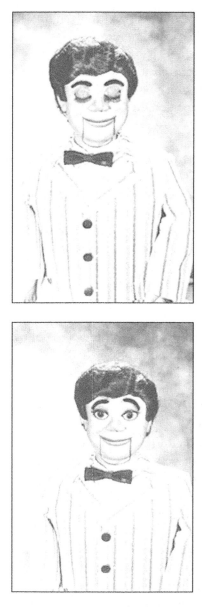

Hard ventriloquial figures are made with a variety of mechanical movements. A movable jaw and head are standard. Three additional movements commonly used are winking or blinking eyes (top left), sticking out the tongue (top right), and movable eyebrows (left).

audience as if for a hint. This type can be screamingly funny for a very short act if the ventriloquist is a good actor.

You will be your own best teacher. By this time you have decided just what kind of character your partner will be. You should be fairly well decided on his voice, and you should now be well on your way to developing a separate personality for him.

Mechanical Manipulation

There is no limit to the number of extra movements that can be installed in a ventriloquial figure. I have seen them with winking eyes, rolling eyes, cross eyes, movable eyebrows, fright wigs, movable noses, movable ears, noses that light up, tongues that stick out, upper lips that move, and with spitting and crying attachments. Other figures have moving arms and legs, and some are even able to walk. While there is no doubt that you can get laughs from all of these unusual actions, you are not helping your reputation as a ventriloquist. You are just the owner of a very expensive example of someone else's ingenuity.

I'm not opposed to some extra movement—if they are not overdone. But don't do what I saw one performer do. He had the figure's eyes rolling, eyelids closing, and opening, and eyebrows moving up and down constantly. It was very confusing, but not so confusing that I didn't hear some rather audible comments around me in regard to the performer's lack of lip control.

You want to be a ventriloquist, and to do so you must create the illusion of life in the figure, so don't make a mechanical doll out of it. Judiciously used, a wink or roll of the eyes, or a smiling upper lip can add a lot to the dialogue, in the way of emphasizing a point. It can get extra laughs for you and add to the figure's personality.

Here is an example. Windy winks at a girl in the front row, to my right. This usually gets a giggle or reaction of some sort from her. I look at her, then at Windy, he looks at me and to the front. I resume the conversation as though nothing had happened. He still looks at her every once in a while, all the people around her expecting another wink. After quite an interval, he does it again. This time we get a few laughs. I look at the girl, I look at Windy, he looks at me, then to the front and I pick up the dialogue where I left off.

If I were to ask him why he was winking at the girl, it would immediately be apparent that I had caused him to wink. Because when he looks to the right, I am unable to see his eyes. After several repetitions of the wink, the laughs get louder. Windy knows, and the audience knows, what is causing the laughs, but I never do find out, so the joke is on me. Windy and the audience are having fun at my expense. You can see how a bit like this will help to make the figure life-like and give him a separate personality.

VENTRILOQUIAL   PSYCHOLOGY

When a magician steps in front of his audience, he is indirectly challenging them to pit their intelligence against his skill. If he is good, he wins, but it is a battle all the way. This is not true of a ventriloquist. If he is any good at all, the audience is with him from the start. All of us have enough childhood imagination to want to believe that the little man really talks. For a while we want to forget the cares of the day and lose ourselves in a world of make believe.

I once heard a ventriloquist open his act by making the statement that he was a ventriloquist and would give a hundred dollars to anyone who could see his lips move while the dummy was talking. No one collected the hundred dollars, for with his face straight to the front and using false speech, he went through the act. Like everyone else, I sat through the whole act with my eyes on his mouth. He convinced all of us that he could talk for ten minutes without moving his lips, but there were very few laughs, and only a polite clapping of hands when he was finished. That's all. Don't challenge your audience, don't call yourself a ventriloquist, and don't call your partner a dummy—at least not in public.

Most of your audience will automatically start to watch the figure as soon as he speaks, but there will be a few critical people who will watch your lips at first. If they see no movement, then they enter into the spirit of the act and you are safe. The only time an audience is critical of a ventriloquist's technique is at the beginning of the act.

I could safely offer a hundred dollars to anyone who could see my lips move for the first two minutes of my act, and I don't use false speech. The words for the figure have been carefully selected, there are no labials, and on two of his lines, I'm wearing a wide smile while he is speaking. I don't hear him the first time, so he repeats it. I turn to him and apologize for not paying attention. I am still smiling and he says, "Who does he think he is, the star of this act?"

All this can be done without any lip movement. By this time your audience is convinced you don't move your lips and they are ready to pay attention to the figure when he speaks. About half way through the act this idea is used again, and at the finish we close with a song, each singing an alternate line. Singing a song not only dis-

Ventriloqual figure with moveable arm.

plays the contrast in the two voices, but looks impressive. You will see later, however, that singing is really rather easy.

After you've become proficient in quickly changing from your natural to your vent voice, and back again, try this. Ask your partner a question while he is looking at someone in the front row. Don't finish the question, but quickly have him say to the person he is looking at "You have pretty hair." He then looks back at you and says, "Sorry, I wasn't listening. What did you say?" If it is done right, the illusion is perfect that you were both talking at the same time, but the voice change must be very fast. With practice it will become easy for you.

Misdirection

A magician uses misdirection to lead the audience's eyes away from where the real "trick" is performed. It is done in such a subtle way that no one sees the trick or realizes they were guided by the magician. A ventriloquist does the same thing by guiding the audience's eyes away from his mouth and toward the figure. In this way he can pronounce difficult words and phrases with full lip movement without detection.

Children from seven to twelve are very critical observers. Before that age, they believe the figure really talks. After that age, most of them are polite enough not to heckle if they see lip movement. But that bunch from seven to twelve will not hesitate to yell, "He ain't alive. I can see you talking for him." So here is where we must use misdirection.

For childrens' shows, I use a standard gag which, although old, never fails to get a laugh. The punch line is "somebody else's pants," which is hard to say. Here is how I handle it.

The whole trend of the act is Windy's trouble at school. He can't spell, he can't add — just what the kids like to hear. So I say, "Windy, I want you to take a little test in addition."

He looks at me and says, "In addition to what?"

I say, "How much is ten and five?"

He answers, "That's a lot."

This has the kids giggling, because he is evading the issue. You will note that so far his words have been easy to pronounce. I say all these lines full face to the audience. When he says, "That's a lot," I get angry. I lean my head over close to his, and tilt it down slightly. I poke my finger on his leg, and I yell, "If you had ten dollars in this pants pocket," I poke the other leg and continue to yell, "and five dollars in this pants pocket, what would you have?"

He yells back, "Somebody else's pants!" I straighten up and give him a very disgusted look and the kids really laugh. I make no attempt to control my lips on that line. I pronounce it clearly and explosively. I have to, because I am yelling in the vent voice. The yelling combined with slightly exaggerated body movement draws the audience's attention to the apparent speaker. The action creates the perfect misdirection and never fails, because it is a natural action for two people who are angry.

If the gag were done quietly, and I turned my head to conceal the lip movement, those people on my extreme right would notice the lip movement.

Misdirection can be used in many ways. It will pay you to try it on an audience, not necessarily that gag, and not necessarily on kids, although they are harder to misdirect than adults.

Movement attracts attention. You see something move out of the corner of your eye and you'll turn to see what it is. You see two or more people together and if only one of them is talking, your eyes will focus on the one moving his lips (if there is no other obvious movement). This is a natural phenomena. When we hear a voice and see only one person's lips moving, our eyes move toward him and mentally associate the voice as coming from those lips.

If you've practiced the techniques I've discussed so far, you should be able to carry on a conversation without much perceptible lip movement. Yet sometimes you will want to make a punch line or statement perfectly clear. Using substitution may not always allow that. This is when you will want to use misdirection.

You can not rely on the movement of the puppet's mouth to always attract attention. The audience knows you are actually doing the talking and will, out of curiosity, look at your lips occasionally.

You will need to make other movements to help draw attention away from your lips. Slow movements do little to help, but sudden jerky moves always draw attention. When done innocently, they provide the perfect misdirection.

THE KEY TO SUCCESS

Practice is essential to success and is the key to learning any skill, but I know of nothing that is more pleasant to practice than ventriloquism. If you follow the system I have outlined, you will show improvement at every practice session. By now you should be getting the impression that your partner is rapidly learning to "talk", he seems more life-like all the time. But you must continue to practice until the voice and lip control, manipulation of the figure, misdirection, and bits of business are second nature to you and require no conscious thought on your part.

Try this to see how far you have advanced: Start a conversation with the figure, not a routine of gags, or anything that you have used before. For instance, you might ask him what he has been doing since you last saw him. The chances are that you will get an answer without any conscious effort on your part. Don't try to be funny. Just keep talking back and forth as long as the illusion seems real to you. When you have to think of an answer for him, quit for a while, but practice talking with your figure every day and you will be surprised how fast you will progress.

Once you can carry on an unrehearsed conversation with your puppet and feel natural doing it, you are well on the road to becoming a successful ventriloquist.

Chapter 5

HOW TO THROW YOUR VOICE

Let me start by saying that throwing your voice is more of a gimmick than anything else. No one can really make their voice come out of a closed box or from the other side of the room. That is impossible; what you really do is create the illusion that you are throwing your voice.

In this chapter I will explain how you can make it appear that someone is talking to you from a distance, giving your audience the impression that you are throwing your voice. This is accomplished by using three types of voices (1) the near-distant voice, (2) the distant voice, and (3) the muffled voice.

THE NEAR-DISTANT VOICE

At times during your act, your partner may not be right next to you when he speaks; he may be temporarily sitting on a chair nearby, in an open box, or leaning away from you. Since he is farther away from the microphone then you are, his voice should sound different.

In this situation you would use the near-distant voice. The puppet is near you but farther away then normal. You "throw your voice" only a short distance.

Creating the near-distant voice is relatively easy. All you need to do to set up this illusion is to adjust the volume of your ventriloquial voice, speaking louder when your partner is close to you and the microphone, and softer as he moves away.

Here is an example of how you can use the near-distant voice to heighten the illusion that the sound comes from the figure. Gradually let him lean away from the microphone. At the same time, his voice gets fainter because you are speaking in a softer vent voice. He does this without you noticing it. Do not mumble. The words should be clear but faint. As soon as you notice this, touch his shoulder. He looks at you and you say, "Get closer to the microphone." Bring his mouth to the mike until he almost touches it. As loud as your vent voice will allow yell, "LIKE THIS?"

If it is a sensitive mike, it will blast the audience almost out of their seats, so you caution him not to get too close and push him back to the proper position. He says, "How's this?" And you say, "Thanks, that's good," and resume the act.

I think you can realize just from reading this bit how effective it is. It never fails to get a hand from the audience, but if it is overdone, it loses its effectiveness. Once during the act is enough for an adult audience.

Another idea is to catch the voice inside a paper bag, a cup, or your closed hands. Using the near-distant voice it can then be released for a comic effect.

THE DISTANT VOICE

The distant voice is used when the ventriloquist is talking to someone who is outside the window, down the stairs, off the stage, or across the room. Since the voice is coming from a distance, it is spoken softer than your own voice and in a slightly higher pitch.

Proficiency with the distant voice is a valuable asset. After you are able to do a good job making the figure talk while close to you, it isn't too difficult to produce the voice as though it's coming from a distance.

Quite a few years ago in a small town, I met a farmer who told me of his uncle, the greatest "voice thrower" who ever lived. He said he could "throw" his voice a mile or more. Seeing that he was serious, I asked how he learned to do this. The farmer said his uncle went out into the field and tried to pick up a tree trunk or rock that was too heavy for him. As he was straining, he talked and that was how he learned.

The man's uncle had discovered for himself the principle of the distant voice, or "voice throwing." You won't have to lift a heavy weight to learn the distant voice, but you will use that principle. Tighten your stomach muscles, tighten your throat, expel the air from your lungs and say "hello" as far back in the throat as possible. This will sound guttural and will appear as though it is coming from your chest.

Do this just enough to familiarize yourself with the feeling. Then try the voice you have been using for the figure, first in the usual way, then by tightening the vocal cords a little and speaking in a slightly higher pitch and forming the word farther back in the mouth. You will hear your figure speaking to you from a distance.

Don't overdo your practice, and don't be in too big a hurry perfect this technique. It is more difficult to do than the figure voice, and it's easy to strain the vocal cores, so take it easy.

When attempting to throw your voice, your lip control and pronunciation must be perfect because the figure is not there to attract attention. It takes a bit of acting to make it convincing. Focus your attention in the direction the voice is supposed to be coming from and make your actions as realistic as possible.

There are several ways to use the distant voice in an act. For example, you can use it to create an echo or loudspeaker effect. "Attention . . . tention . . . tention . . . tention, all K-Mart shoppers . . . oppers . . . oppers . . . oppers."

Another approach is to tell your partner that the place is haunted. There is a ghost in the cellar. Of course he doubts this, so you lean over and shout toward the floor "Who's down there?" And the distant voice comes back "Who wants to know?" You say to the figure, "Go on, tell him who wants to know."

But your partner is frightened. He wants to get away from the ghost, so you tell him it isn't really a ghost, merely an echo. He then wants to know what an echo is, so you explain by saying, "Hello" in your natural voice. In reply you get a "Hello" in your distant voice. The figure looks at you quickly and says, "You did that."

You deny it and tell him to try it. He yells. "Hello" in a loud voice, then appears to listen, but nothing happens. He says to you, "See, it's fake." Just then you say "Hello" in the figure's distant voice and startled he jumps.

This bit is especially effective if you both whisper when talking about the ghost. You will find that, even when whispering you can maintain a definite contrast between your voice and the figure's voice.

You should not attempt to learn the distant voice and voice throwing until you have perfected the voice for the figure. For one thing the figure's voice is easier to learn than the distant voice. After you have mastered the figure's voice the transition to the distant voice will not seem difficult. Another important reason is that some friend who knows of your study in ventriloquism may ask you to demonstrate your "voice throwing" in a group. If you have only a smattering of what to do, it will be a sorry exhibition. After all, you know as well as I do that friends and relatives are your severest critics. What they say may discourage you from further practice.

It is much better to become proficient in doing ventriloquism with the figure. After people have had a chance to see your skill, and after you have mastered the distant voice, then will be the time to "throw your voice."

An alibi which helped me in the early days was to tell my friends that since I didn't have too much experience, I could only throw my voice as far as the figure. Any greater distance was too much of a strain.

There are certain conditions under which the distant voice illusion cannot be produced. Never attempt to produce the distant voice on the other side of your audience. It would be impossible.

Of course, you and I know that no one can actually throw the voice, but since the public speaks of ventriloquism in this way and since the idea is widely believed, you should never disillusion them. The fact that people believe the voice is actually being thrown makes a ventriloquist seem that much better.

THE MUFFLED VOICE

The muffled voice is used when you talk to your partner or someone who is in a closed box, truck, bag, in a closet, or behind a door. It is different from the near-distant voice in that it is slightly smothered.

The muffled sound can be made simply by pushing your tongue against the back of your teeth as you speak. Recite the following sentences using the muffled voice:

It's dark in here.
Let me out.
I can't see.
Hello out there.
Open that door.

Here is an example of how you can use the muffled voice. Lean over, rap the top of the box with your knuckles, and say "Hello." Kick the back of the box with your toe and answer "Hello" in the distant voice, then carry on a short conversation with the person in the box.

When talking to someone standing behind a door you would face the door and call out, "Who's there?" The answer would have to be more distant than the voice from the box or the trunk. If the voice were to come from under a couch, then it would be both distant and muffled as a person's voice really would sound muffled by the carpet and by the cloth in the couch. If you were talking to someone on the phone, the voice coming over the receiver will be muffled.

During the show a pesky fly can annoy the performer. The audience can not see the fly but they can hear the "zzzzz" it makes and see the performer's efforts to shoo it away. He can succeed in grabbing the little troublemaker in his hands and then have it plead to be let go leading into a fly-human conversation. The performer talking to his clasped hands and acting as if the fly's voice is coming from inside.

Chapter 6

VENTRILOQUIAL GIMMICKS

VOCAL SOUNDS

Your partner can make a wide variety of sounds beside speech. Using other sounds occasionally will add personality and reinforce the realness of the puppet. You should learn how to make your partner whisper, cry, snore, cough, hiccup, sneeze, mumble, and laugh. Most of these sounds are easy to make ventriloquially; all you need to do is make the sound and add an appropriate action.

If you want your partner to whisper, bring his mouth to your ear, soften the voice, and talk in a raspy tone.

At times you may want your partner to cry. Some vent figures are made so that water can be squirted out of the eyes, simulating tears. Cry in your vent voice and put his head on your shoulder, or bend his head forward and shake it slowly back and forth.

If you want him to sleep, bend his head down so the eyes are not visible and make a snoring sound. Raise and lower him slightly with each breath.

When your partner coughs, open and close his mouth quickly while jerking his head forward.

To give him hiccups, quickly open and close his mouth while jerking his head back slightly.

Your figure can yawn by leaning back, opening his mouth, and making a yawning sound.

Try these and other vocal sounds with the action that would natur-ally accompany them. Be careful not to overdo the movement your partner makes or the action may appear unnatural. Using a mirror while practicing will help.

SINGING

Having your partner sing a song or singing a duet with him is a technique commonly used by ventriloquists. It adds variety to your act and displays your skill, all to the delight of the audience. Most any type of song can be used. Humorous songs are particularly good.

Singing in your vent voice is really no harder than talking, and in some cases it's easier. If the song is a familiar one, the audience will mentally sing along with you. They will anticipate each word in the song and will not notice the slight variations in pronunciation your partner makes in some of the words.

When you sing a duet it becomes even easier because you sing alternate lines. In your natural voice you sing the lines containing the labials, and the figure sings the easy lines. To the public, singing a duet looks hard. They assume that it is harder to "throw the voice" while singing.

DRINKING

If you are interested in selling yourself as an expert ventriloquist, the ability to drink or eat while the figure is speaking will add to your reputation.

If you propose to make a living personality out of the figure, the less you say about stunts the better, for if the figure were alive, there would be nothing remarkable about his talking while you were eating or drinking.

These stunts are used by me at different times, but never for the same audience. They are worked in as natural actions. For drinking, you can buy a trick glass at most any magic shop. The glass appears to be full, but holds only has about an ounce of liquid. As it is held

to the lips and tilted, the liquid goes into a double well. The level of the liquid goes down about 75% and it appears as though it went into your mouth, and will not interfere with your speech.

I use one of these glasses. It is about four inches tall and is made of very thick glass. Although it looks like it holds a lot of liquid, it only holds a little over an ounce. I fill it with Coca-Cola and let it sit until the gas has evaporated. When my partner is singing, I pick up the glass and as he sustains the last note, I force the sound through my nose, put the glass to my lips and slowly pour the liquid into my mouth.

It is important to keep your chin up. The liquid is actually held in your mouth. While holding one note in the song, the tongue is not moving. It is surprising how much liquid you can hold in your mouth. After the glass is empty and while the figure is holding the last note, smile, and as the note finishes, close the lips, the figure and you both take a bow, and you incline your head forward and swallow the liquid.

EATING

Very few ventriloquists have mastered the technique of eating while the figure is talking. Here is the way I do it. Windy, my partner, has an apple in his pocket. I take it out and start to take a bite. He objects because he wants to take it to his teacher. (There's

It's the skill of illusion that transforms puppets into animated characters.

room here for a bit of comedy.) I open my mouth wide to bite the apple, but slide my teeth over the surface of the apple and merely take a small bite. The piece of apple is forced in the side of the mouth between the cheek and the teeth. I now speak in a natural voice, as though my mouth is full. When Windy speaks, I take pains to make his pronunciation particularly clear. This is very effective.

Of course I have to get rid of the apple before I take too many bites, so I mention how tasty the apple is and ask him where he got it. He replies that he found it in the street. I give him a disgusted look and throw the apple off the stage.

Chapter 7

HOW TO CREATE
YOUR OWN DIALOGUES

READY-MADE DIALOGUES

Good ventriloquial technique is not enough to make you a successful puppeteer or ventriloquist. A funny dialogue is also essential. Watching a puppet talk is interesting, but not particularly entertaining. You must have a story or humorous patter if your audience is to enjoy the act.

Where do you get material for a dialogue? If you would like a ready-made dialogue there are several books available just for that purpose. You can find dialogue books at local puppet and magic shops, or order them by mail from dealers who carry puppet supplies. Addresses for several mail order suppliers are listed in the appendix. I have also provided samples of several dialogues at the end of this book to help get you started.

At first you may try the dialogues in this book or buy some dialogue books. You do not have to use a complete dialogue as it is written. You will be more successful if you combine several dialogues, using only the funniest lines and adapting the material to you and your partner's personalities.

It is important that both of you have well defined personalities and that you stay in character as you perform. No matter how funny a joke is, don't use it unless it fits your personality. For example, if your partner plays an ignorant country bumpkin, don't have him pull a clever joke on you, or make you look stupider than he is, at least not on purpose. This type of character can come out ahead, but it should appear to be by accident, not by design.

BUILDING A JOKE FILE

You can use ready-made dialogues, but writing your own material is best. Original material will fit your personalities and type of humor better. This doesn't mean that you have to create all of your jokes from scratch (that would be a difficult task) but you should use a variety of sources and combine the most appropriate material to form your dialogue.

Where do you get jokes and story ideas? Everywhere. Humor is all around us in books, newspapers, TV, radio, magazines, and personal conversations.

Get a folder, file, or box and start now to collect jokes. This will be your joke file. Whenever you come across something that strikes you as funny, write it down and file it. Arrange the jokes in order by topic for easy reference. Most all writers and comedians keep journals or files such as this. So should you. In this way you will have a ready-made source of jokes to use when you need a new joke or a new script.

WRITING A SCRIPT

Writing your own script is not as hard as you might believe. If you follow the guidelines I will give you, then you will be able to produce interesting new scripts like a professional comedy writer.

The first step in writing a script is to decide on a theme or topic. Once you have chosen a topic, adding comic dialogue is simple.

Your next step is to get you joke file and locate all the jokes that would fit the topic you chose. For example, if the topic you chose was school, the jokes you may choose might be about reading, writing, arithmetic, teaches, classmates, playground games, or homework.

Your script will be organized into three parts (1) a beginning or introduction, (2) the main body of the dialogue, and (3) an ending.

The beginning introduces you to the audience and lets them know a little bit about you and what type of act to expect.

The main body of your dialogue is composed of a series of jokes. Look at your joke file and select several appropriate jokes. Starting with your introduction begin stringing the jokes together. You may need to use a transition sentence to flow smoothly from one joke to the next.

Make your routine snappy and fast-paced. Don't risk boring the audience with unnecessary dialogue. Eliminate all nonessential words. As you build your script, concentrate on getting the greatest number of laughs with the fewest words.

End your routine with your funniest gag. Closing with a big laugh will earn you greater applause and leave the audience wanting more (rather than being glad you're quitting). When you're finished, end with a closing statement. Ending with "That's all, thanks" is like pulling the chair out from under the audience and letting them drop with a jolt. Instead, let them down gently with a closing statement which gives a reason for the conversation to stop.

Here's an example of how I would build a short dialogue using this method.

First I must choose a topic. For this example the topic I will use is "visiting a farm." I then look in my joke file under "farm," "work," "gardens," "animals," and any other related subject I might have. Several jokes are selected. Here are four jokes I have chosen for this example, exactly as they appear in my joke file:

Joke #1
Abner: We've got a hen down at our house that lays white eggs.
Luke: What's so wonderful about that?
Abner: Can you do it?

Joke #2
First Neighbor: What were all your chickens doing out in front of
    your house early this morning?

Second Neighbor: They heard some men were going to lay a sidewalk and they wanted to see how it was done.

Joke #3

Farm Boy: My pop can't decide whether to get a new cow or a tractor for his farm.

City Boy: He'd certainly look silly riding around on a cow.

Farm Boy: Yeah, but he would look a lot sillier milking a tractor!

Joke #4

A man dropped in to pay a friend an unexpected visit, and was amazed to find him playing chess with his dog. The man watched in silence for a few minutes, then burst out with: "That's the smartest dog I ever saw in my life!"

Oh, he isn't so smart," was the answer. "I've beaten him three games out of five."

Next I arrange the jokes in a logical sequence, using a transition sentence wherever needed. Rarely is a joke used exactly as it was written in my file. To make the jokes fit into the dialogue I usually have to reword them, being careful not to destroy the effect of the punch line. I end with a simple closing statement.

The following dialogue is the result.

Introduction

Ventriloquist: Hello, my name is _____. And this is my friend Elmo Piggins.

Elmo: Hi folks! That's me, Elmo Piggins.

V: Whoa, Elmo, don't get so excited.

E: I can't help it. I just got back from visiting my grandpa's farm.

Transition

V: Oh, I see. He does have a lot of interesting animals doesn't he?

Joke #1

E: I'll say. He has a hen that lays white eggs.

V: What's so wonderful about that?
E: Can YOU do it?

Transition
V: Did you get to see many chickens?

Joke #2
E: No, they were all down by the street.
V: How come?
E: They heard that some men were going to lay a sidewalk and they wanted to see how it was done.

Transition
V: Does your grandpa still use that old tractor of his?

Joke #3
E: Yeah. He can't decide whether to get a new cow or a tractor.
V: He'd certainly look silly riding around on a cow.
E: Yeah, but he would look a lot sillier milking a tractor!

Transition
V: What does your grandpa do for fun?

Joke #4
E: He plays chess with his dog Snorf.
V: What! You mean to tell me his dog can play chess? Why that must be the smartest dog in the world!
E: Oh, he ain't so smart. I beat him three games out of five.

Ending and Final Laugh
V: Well you're not so smart either. Look what you stepped in.
E: (Bends over to look at the bottom of his shoe.) OOOOOH! (The figure's reaction can be supplemented with mechanical movements such as spinning his head in a full circle, lifting it above his shoulders, or sticking out his tongue. This bit of physical comedy

compounds the humor of the incident, creating a perfect ending.)
V: (Holding his nose and making a sour face.) I think we better go
now.

After you've written a rough draft of your script, go back over it
and read the parts, using your vent voice. Modify the script so you
don't overburden yourself with difficult words.

While the whole dialogue may seem very funny to you, some gags
will fall flat. This may not be the fault of the dialogue. It may be your
delivery of the lines.

Remember the lines that get the biggest laughs. Eventually you
will combine the best lines from several sources. When you do, you
will be able to get many more laughs. Keep eliminating the weakest
lines and substituting stronger ones all the time.

Eventually this will be your number one act. As soon as you are

Children love animal figures.

satisfied, start building a number two act for return appearances.

Some performers have the figure talk more than they do. One very successful performer says only about one third of the words in the dialogue, but he is an exception, as it is more difficult to sustain the vent voice for a long sentence. Also, if the audience has a chance to listen to the vent voice too long, it begins to sound like the performer's voice.

Another thing to remember is that the figure is the star of the act. What he says is important, so don't force him to use a lot of extra words to build up the gag. On the other hand, don't make the mistake of being too long-winded yourself in leading up to the punch line.

In my act, I have Windy inject a word now and then if I am using a rather long gag. At the end of a sentence he will say "Yes, go on" or "You are so right." This keeps him from sitting too long and also keeps the audience conscious of the contrast in the two voices.

When writing your scripts make sure your dialogs fit the personality and character of your puppets. A dialog designed for a smart aleck kid may not go over well using another type of figure. Also keep in mind the type of audience you are writing for. Will it be a group of children or adults? Perhaps it will be a group of boy scouts or a nursery school full of five-year-olds. Each audience will be somewhat different . This arc just a few things to be aware of as you write your scripts.

If you feel you need help creating your own comic material, I suggest reading the book *Creative Clowning*. This book discusses in detail how to generate ideas and write your own funny scripts. It's a valuable reference for any puppeteer's library. *Creative Clowning* can be purchased at your local magic or puppet shop or ordered directly from the publisher of the book you are now reading (see copyright page for contact information). Additional ideas for developing your own scripts can be found in Maher Studios' booklet *Writing Your Own Scripts* and Stephen Axtell's *Jokestorming Techniques*.

Chapter 8

COMIC DIALOGUES

Many novice puppeteers and ventriloquists need a little help creating their own scripts. For this reason I have included several practice dialogues in this book.

Just reading about ventriloquism won't make you a ventriloquist. As in any skill, you must practice. Besides providing you with some material to start with, these dialogues can also be of great assistance in helping you develop your ventriloquial skills. Get your figure and this book, and both of you read them together.

In your normal voice, read the ventriloquist's lines; then in your vent voice, read your partner's. You and your puppet may not have the same personality as depicted here, but reading the dialogues will help teach you to shift back and forth from your natural voice to your vent voice.

Read the dialogues with meaning. Be an actor. Use full expression and emotion. Make your partner as realistic as you possibly can.

I would suggest that you read each of these dialogues many times, and even memorize a few. Try them out in front of a mirror to check your lip movement, and use a tape recorder to evaluate your pronunciation and delivery.

If you do this I have no doubt that you will develop a skill that will be respected and admired by your audiences and bring you the joys shared by other ventriloquists and puppeteers.

This chapter is divided into two major sections. In the first section I have provided several dialogues which were used on the Holsum

TV show with Windy Higgins. These are classic dialogues in that Windy plays a smart aleck boy who always comes up with the witty humor. The second half of this chapter consists of dialogues using novelty figures.

CLASSIC DIALOGUES

Higgins is the Name
(Announcer introduces Windy.)
Windy: That's me, Windy Higgins (wink).
Paul: Hi!
W: Hi, boys and girls.
P: Don't you know it's impolite to interrupt someone while they're talking?
W: Well, who are you?
P: I'm Paul Stadelman, Magician.
W: O.K. Let's see you disappear.
P: You talked so much and interrupted the announcer, I think I should introduce you again.
W: Go ahead.
P: Boys and girls, this is my little friend, Windy Higgins.
W: That's me, that's us!
P: Don't say "That's us," you'll get the people mixed up and they won't know which one is the dummy.
W: It is hard to tell.
P: I want these boys and girls to know that I don't make a living by acting dumb.
W: No, you do it for nothing.
P: Why don't you introduce yourself?
W: How do you do it?
P: Just tell them your name.
W: The whole thing?
P: Sure, go ahead.
W: Windy L. Higgins
P: What's the "L" for?

W: Lassie.
P: Lassie?
W: Yea, daddy wanted a dog.
P: What's your daddy's name?
W: Higgins.
P: What's his first name?
W: Higgins.
P: That's silly. How could his name be Higgins Higgins?
W: He stutters.
P: Tell us your father's first name.
W: I really don't know.
P: Well, what does your mother call him?
W: Huh?
P: I said what does your mother call your father?
W: Oh, no, I couldn't say that on television.
P: Well, where do you live?
W: With me.
P: Then where do you and your daddy live?
W: Together.
P: You are a smart aleck, little boy. If you were my son, I'd give
   you poison.
W: If you were my daddy, I'd take it.
P: Windy, How do you like being on television?
W: It's all right except for the lights.
P: What's wrong with the lights?
W: The lights hurt my eyes.
P: You don't have to look at the lights. You can look at me.
W: That hurts worse.
P: That's all for you. Behind the screen!

Arithmetic Quiz
Windy: That's me. Windy Higgins (long wink).
Paul: Hi, boys and girls.
W: Hi, sure glad to be back on the Holsum Show.
P: Say, Windy, you got a lot of mail.
W: I did?

P: Yes sir. One little girl wants to know if you go to school.
W: Let's don't talk about that.
P: Well, you do go to school, don't you?
W: Well, I do when I can't get out of it.
P: And just what are you taking at school?
W: Anything that ain't nailed down.
P: That sounds like you steal. You don't, do you?
W: No. I just find things before they get lost.
P: And what is your favorite study?
W: Recess!
P: I have a note from your teacher. She said you got into a fight and kicked a little boy in the stomach. I don't like to hear those things.
W: Then you shouldn't listen.
P: Well, did you kick him in the stomach?
W: Well, yea and no. It was an accident. He turned around a little too quick.
P: She said your arithmetic was bad. Maybe I should give you a little test.
W: I don't need it.
P: You're going to get it. How much is two and two?
W: What's that? Two and two?
P: That's what I said.
W: That's what I thought you said.
P: Well, what is it?
W: Twenty-two.
P: It is not.
W: (Mumbling.) Write it down and you'll see.
P: I'll give you a hint. If you had two apples—
W: I don't like apples.
P: I don't care if you like them or not. If you had two apples and I gave you two more—
W: You wouldn't give them to me.
P: Oh, yes, I would.
W: Then they wouldn't be fit to eat.
P: Quit stalling. How much is two apples and two apples?

W: Sixteen.

P: That's too many.

W: Three.

P: That's not enough

W: You're hard to please.

P: All right. I'll tell you. Two apples and two apples would be four apples.

W: Did you say apples?

P: I sure did.

W: Shucks. I was figuring with oranges. Say Paul, what is two and two?

P: Why, four, of course. Don't you know I went to school, stupid?

W: Yeah, and you came out the same way!

P: Into the woodshed for you!

The Circus

Paul: Windy, you told me last week Uncle Eddie was going to take you to the circus. Did he?

Windy: He sure did and what a day! He bought me an all day sucker.

P: That little piece of candy you brought home was an all-day sucker?

W: Yeah. Uncle Eddie says the days are getting shorter all the time.

P: What else did he buy you?

W: A hot dog, but it made me sick.

P: Well, I ate one of those hot dogs and it was all right.

W: Well, the first six were all right, but the seventh was bad.

P: He should know better then to buy you seven hot dogs. It's a wonder he didn't buy a dozen.

W: He couldn't.

P: Why?

W: I ran out of money.

P: Did you see the India Rubber Man in the side show?

W: Yeah, and could he stretch his skin. He had more wrinkles, than you.

P: These are not wrinkles. They are dimples.
W: They're the longest dimples I ever saw.
P: What did the India Rubber Man say to you?
W: I couldn't understand him. He's a foreigner.
P: I think he is a Czechoslovakian.
W: Oh, a Rubber Check!
P: Did you see the elephant?
W: The big thing with a tail on each end?
P: No, no. The one in front is his trunk.
W: I guess the other one is his suit case.
P: Do you know in what country the elephant is found?
W: I don't even know in what country they are lost.
P: What else did you see?
W: I saw the old kangaroo crying cause her little one ran away.
P: Really?
W: Yeah. He left her holding the bag.
P: What else?
W: We never did find the Dangaroos.
P: What is that?
W: I don't know. The sign said, Dangeroos — Keep Away!"
P: How was it spelled?
W: D-A-N-G-E-R-O-U-S.
P: That's dangerous. Uncle Eddie should have told you what it
    was.
W: He couldn't. He was in the monkey cage.
P: How did he get in there?
W: I don't know, there he was.
P: Wouldn't they let him out?
W: No. They couldn't tell which one was Uncle Eddie.
P: Say, Windy, did you know my father was an animal trainer?
W: What did he teach you?
P: That's all for you — into the woodshed!

Hotel Life
Paul: Windy, still more mail, and all of these children ask questions
    about you.

Windy: Nosey, aren't they?

P: Oh, I don't think so. Here's a boy who wants to know where you live.

W: I live at the (mumble, mumble) Hotel.

P: I didn't understand the name of the hotel.

W: Not supposed to. It's censored.

P: I guess you have room and bath?

W: Is this Saturday?

P: At least you have running water in your room?

W: Yeah, the roof leaks.

P: No, no. I mean, you have hot and cold water in your room.

W: Huh?

P: I said you have two kinds of water in your room.

W: Yeah, clean and dirty.

P: Do they ask much for the room rent?

W: Yeah, two or three times a day.

P: I mean, what do you pay for the room?

W: Two.

P: Two dollars?

W: Naw, too darned much.

P: That was an awful racket in the hotel last night.

W: That was the night clerk.

P: What was he doing?

W: Kicking my pants down the stairs.

P: I never heard a pair of pants make that much noise.

W: I was still in them.

P: Did you get hurt?

W: Sure. I got infernal injuries.

P: You mean internal. Infernal means the lower regions.

W: Where do you think I got kicked?

P: Do you still stay there?

W: No, I am an extinguished guest.

P: You mean "distinguished" guest. "Extinguished" means "put out."

W: That's me.

P: I ate at the coffee shop in your hotel.

W: Do you think you'll live?

P: It wasn't too bad, except I found a fly in my soup.
W: Well, how much soup can a fly drink.
P: Another customer found a needle in his soup.
W: That was a typographical error. It should have been a noodle.
P: And that little dog sitting there worried me. He kept looking
    at me all the time I was eating.
W: You were eating out of his plate.
P: Why didn't you tell me?
W: I didn't care. He wasn't my dog.

Kids and Goats
Windy: That's me, Windy Higgins.
Paul: Hi, everybody. This is Paul Stadelman, the personality boy
    (smile).
W: Did you say boy?
P: Yeah, I said boy. Why don't you say "Hi" to our visitors.
W: Hi, kids.
P: Ah, ah, uh, uh, you must not say"kids." That infers that they
    are goats.
W: Say, Paul, how's your kid?
P: You mean my lovely child Ronnie?
W: Well, if you put it that way, all right. What does he eat?
P: He doesn't eat. He drinks goat's milk.
W: Did you say goat's milk?
P: That's right. Goat's milk. It is very expensive.
W: Why don't you get a goat?
P: Where'd we keep him?
W: Under your bed.
P: What about the smell?
W: Oh, he'd get used to it.
P: How do we get into these things?
W: I asked you how your kid was.
P: Yes.
W: You said "Don't call him a kid."
P: Right.
W: He drinks goat's milk?

P: Right again.
W: Say, Paul, how's your kid?
P: Don't be so facetious.
W: Never touch the stuff.

The Questionaire

Windy: Did I get any letters?
Paul: Quite a few. Here is one I'd like to read to you.
W: Who is it from?
P: It's from Washington.
W: Cut out the kidding. He's dead.
P: This is Washington, D.C.
W: Oh, I see.
P: No, D.C. Do you know what that means?
W: Sure. Darned crowded.
P: Do you know what this is?
W: Sure. It's a Frigidaire.
P: No, it's a questionaire. A Frigidaire freezes things.
W: Well, I got cold feet when I saw it.
P: There are a lot of questions to be filled out, so I'll help you,
   if you'll lend me your pencil.
W: I ain't got no pencil.
P: That's a double negative.
W: You mean I ain't got two pencils?
P: No, no. To use proper English, you should say: I have no
   pencil, she has no pencil, he has no pencil." Do you
   understand?
W: Sure. There ain't nobody got no pencils.
P: Your grammar is terrible.
W: She is not. She is a nice old lady.
P: Come on, let's fill it out. What name should I put down?
W: Paul Stadelman.
P: That's me.
W: I know. You go. I don't want to.
P: So I'll put down Windy Higgins.
W: You sure are generous with my life.

P: Born?
W: Certainly. You think I'm a dummy?
P: No, no. Where were you born?
W: Upstairs.
P: In what state were you born?
W: In a state of nudity.
P: What state of the Union?
W: No, no union suit. No clothes at all.
P: Were you born in Illinois?
W: That's right.
P: What part.
W: All of me.
P: Let's see now. Description: dark hair, brown eyes, any scars?
W: Huh?
P: I say, do you have any scars on you?
W: Not even a cigarette.
P: How many brothers and sisters do you have?
W: Two of each.
P: Two brothers, two sisters and you. That makes five children all together.
W: No, one at a time.
P: How old are you?
W: I'm at the awkward age. Too old to cry and too young to cuss! How old are you?
P: Why don't you guess?
W: That's easy. You're fifty.
P: I hate to admit it, but it's true. How did you do it?
W: I got a brother who is twenty five and he is just half crazy.
P: Into the woodshed for you.

New Contract
Paul: Well, Windy, I had a long talk with our sponsor today. He had a lot to say. He told me what he thought of the show.
Windy: Don't worry. We can always get another job.
P: We don't have to. We signed a new contact today.
W: "We" signed a new contract?

P: Well I signed for both of us. You know in an act like this, one of us has to have a brain.

W: Yeah, and I got it.

P: Oh, I wouldn't say that.

W: You don't have to. I just said it.

P: Look, I did all right before I had you. I didn't get rich, but I didn't miss any meals.

W: No, But you postponed a lot.

P: We got a raise on this contract.

W: That won't do me any good.

P: Sure it will. We always go 50-50.

W: Yes, out of each fifty dollars, I get fifty cents. That's your old 50-50.

P: This contract goes for another three years.

W: At your age, you'll never make it.

P: Oh, I'm not so old.

W: I don't know. Even George Burns called you"Mister."

P: I'm in the neighborhood of forty.

W: You should move. You're in the wrong neighborhood.

Spelling Test

Paul: Well, Windy, it's time for school again. I suppose you're happy.

Windy: No, I ain't gonna go any more.

P: And why not?

W: I went last year.

P: I know that, but every year you go you are in a different grade, and you learn different things.

W: I've been in the same grade so long, the other kids think I'm the teacher.

P: You should study, and pay attention to your teacher.

W: She ain't so smart. When she wants to know anything, she has to ask me. What's two and two, and what's three and three and stuff like that.

P: She knows all that. She wants to find out what you know.

W: I ain't talking. I ain't no stool pigeon.

P: Well, what do you have the most trouble with?
W: Gazintas.
P: Oh, what on earth is gazintas?
W: Oh, you know. Two gazinta four, three gazinta six.
P: How's your spelling?
W: Not too good.
P: Let's try an easy little word
W: You try it.
P: No, you try it. There it is: C-A-T.
W: That's right.
P: I know it's right.
W: Who told you?
P: Come on, what does C-A-T spell?
W: Dog.
P: Wrong; Try this: D-O-G.
W: Cat.
P: Wrong. Try this: P-I-P-E.
W: CAT.
P: No, I'll give you a hint. P-I-P-E is something I smoke.
W: Second hand cigars?
P: Here's your last chance. We have a P-I-P-E in our kitchen. It
   runs across the floor, up the wall and down into the sink.
W: Oh, I know. Roaches!
P: I'm ashamed of you. When George Washington was your age,
   he was in the eighth grade.
W: So what. When he was your age, he was president!
P: Into the woodshed!

Show-Biz

Windy: Are you glad you know me?
Paul: Sure I'm glad, but why do you ask?
W: You know I got you on television.
P: Oh, I don't know about that. I could have made it alone.
W: No, You couldn't. You're too old to wrestle.
P: I didn't do so bad in show business before I met you. I didn't
   get rich, but at least I didn't miss any meals.

W: No, but you sure postponed a lot.
P: I was in vaudeville before it died.
W: What's the reason it died?
P: I was a good actor, when I played a death scene, the audience was in tears.
W: Yeah, they knew you weren't really dead.
P: Once I did an Oriental act, and they burned incense.
W: I guess it was a punk act.
P: And my singing was very good. When I sing, I sing from the heart.
W: Say, if you had a heart, you wouldn't sing.
P: And then I took up magic.
W: You should drop it.
P: I stood on the stage and fooled the audience.
W: Yeah, they thought you were alive.
P: The people liked me. They applauded and said, come back, come back.
W: Yeah, one guy dared you to came back.
P: My act was very original.
W: What's that?
P: It was different from the other magicians.
W: Oh, I see. The others were good.
P: You know the old trick of pulling a rabbit from a hat?
W: Sure, let's see you do it.
P: Not right now. I don't have a hat.
W: You don't have a rabbit. That's the reason!
P: Instead of pulling a rabbit from a hat, I used to pull a hat from a rabbit.
W: If you're so good, why aren't you with Houdini?
P: Why, he's dead.
W: I know it.

Aches and Pains
Paul: How are you feeling, Windy?
Windy: Okay, and you?
P: Oh, I can't kick.

W: Rheumatism, eh?
P: Well, I do have a pain in my back. Sort of lumbago.
W: What's that?
P: Lumbago is a pain in the lumbar region.
W: Why didn't you say you had a headache?
P: Well, the doctor gave me a tonic.
W: With iron in it?
P: Yes, how did you know?
W: Your face looks rusty.
P: That doctor saved my life once.
W: You called him and he didn't come?
P: No, he gave me a white pill for my liver and a brown one for my stomach.
W: That's silly. How would they know which way to go?
P: How is your health?
W: Oh, fine, fine.
P: Were you ever troubled by diphtheria?
W: Only when I tried to spell it.
P: You know diseases are caused by germs, and deep breathing will kill germs.
W: How you gonna get a germ to breathe deep?
P: I heard Uncle Eddie is in the hospital.
W: That's right.
P: What for?
W: Three weeks.
P: No, no, did he have an operation?
W: Sure did.
P: What did they operate for?
W: Three hundred dollars.
P: I mean, what did he have?
W: Two hundred and fifty dollars.
P: What was his complaint?
W: The bill was too high.
P: Tell me, what was he sick of?
W: Operations.
P: Did they take his temperature.

W: Was it missing?
P: Stop kidding. What was the real reason Uncle Eddie was in the hospital?
W: His girl friend shot him.
P: At close range?
W: What's that?
P: Did he have powder marks on his clothes?
W: Sure. That's the reason she shot Him!
P: That's enough. To the woodshed for you.

Out of Work
Windy: That's me, Windy Higgins.
Paul: Hi, everybody, this is Paul Stadelman, the Ventriloquial Virtuoso.
W: Say that again.
P: I won't do it.
W: You can't do it. I dare you.
P: I said this is Paul Stadelman, Ventuodo Virtro. . . oh, you have me all mixed up.
W: You were mixed up before I knew you.
P: I'm surprised to see you here today.
W: Why, this is Tuesday. I work here on Tuesday.
P: Not any more. You were fired after last week's show. You insulted Uncle Eddie.
W: I only say what you think.
P: Any how, you're fired.
W: That's news to me.
P: They sent you a letter from WBKB, saying you were fired. Didn't you get it?
W: Oh, I got that. It said on the envelope, "Return in five days to WBKB," so here I am.
P: Well, I don't need you any more, so good-bye.
W: I'll go and get a job with Victor Grinnell.
P: Who is Victor Grinnell?
W: He's a ventriloquist and a good one, too!
P: I never heard of him.

W: He has heard of you.

P: I expect he has.

W: And you should hear what he says about you!

P: Never mind that. If you are going to look for a job, you should be neat and comb your hair.

W: No.

P: No, what?

W: No comb.

P: Then borrow Uncle Eddie's

W: He doesn't have one.

P: How does he comb his hair?

W: He hasn't got any.

P: You are making that up. He is not bald.

W: No, he's just a little too tall for his hair.

P: His hair is a little thin.

W: Who wants fat hair?

P: Didn't Uncle Eddie used to work in a bank?

W: Till he got fired.

P: Why?

W: They caught him taking samples.

P: What's he doing now?

W: Ten years.

P: If you would stop making up those ridiculous stories about Uncle Eddie and be a good boy, I'll see if I can get your job back.

W: That's fine, I like you. You're a good guy.

P: I like you, too, Windy, and if I have said anything to offend you, I'm sorry.

W: What's that?

P: I'm sorry.

W: You certainly are. You're the sorriest character I ever saw.

P: That did it. Into the woodshed with you, silver lips.

The Wizard of Ahs

Windy: That's me, Windy Higgins.

Paul: Hi, everybody, this is Paul Stadelman, the Wizard of Ahs.

(pause) I'll repeat that. The Wizard of Ahs.

W: That's old stuff. I read that story.

P: You are thinking of the Wizard of Oz. O-Z. Oz. Mine is spelled A-H-S, Ahs.

W: So what.

P: That's what the audience says when I do magic."Ah!"

W: Ah, nuts, you're not so good.

P: Neither are you. That was pretty bad the way you sang School Days last week. You can't sing.

W: That's your fault.

P: I have a good voice. It's been cultivated.

W: It should be plowed under.

P: I think I sing very well.

W: You sound like a cow.

P: I resent that. I get a thousand dollars a week for singing, does that sound like cow?

W: No, bull.

P: Suppose I pick on you for a while.

W: Go ahead. You can't win.

P: You were late to school yesterday.

W: That's on account of the sign in front of the school.

P: What sign?

W: It says, "School—Go Slowly."

P: That sign is not for you. You should always try to be early. Remember, it's the early bird that gets the worm.

W: I don't want a worm.

P: Well, I can't win. Let's go to the woodshed.

Columbus Day

Windy: That's me, Windy Higgins.

Paul: Say, so you know what the day after tomorrow is?

W: Sure, Thursday.

P: That's right. But it's also Columbus Day.

W: So?

P: Don't you know about Columbus.

W: Sure. Columbus, Ohio.

P: No, his name was Christopher Columbus.
W: Aw, that was his maiden name.
P: Columbus discovered America. Do you know how?
W: Sure, he just looked and there it was.
P: Before he made his trip, everyone thought the world was flat.
W: I always thought it was crooked.
P: What is the shape of the world?
W: It's a mess.
P: That's not the right answer.
W: Don't you listen to the radio.
P: Here's a hint. What shape are my cuff buttons?
W: Square.
P: The ones I wear on Sunday are square, but what shape are the ones I wear on week days?
W: Round.
P: Now you have it. What's the shape of the world?
W: Round on week days, square on Sunday.
P: Your geography is bad. You should study it more.
W: It's changing too fast.
P: What is the Capitol of the United States?
W: About half what it used to be.
P: Where is the Capitol of the United States?
W: Most of it's in Japan.
P: Do you know when Columbus discovered America?
W: No, I wasn't there.
P: Here is a little poem that will help you. In 1492 Columbus sailed the ocean blue.
W: Say, that's easy
P: Sure it is. Now what was the date?
W: 1493.
P: Have you forgotten the poem?
W: No. In 1493, Columbus sailed the deep blue sea.
P: I give up. Let's go to the woodshed.

Report Card
Windy: That's me, Windy Higgins.

Paul: Hi, everybody, this is Paul Stadelman, the Wistful Wit of Wonderland.

W: What did you say?

P: I said "wit."

W: That's what I thought you said.

P: Don't you think I'm right?

W: At least you're half right, half wit.

P: I'm nobody's fool

W: Nobody will have you.

P: Here is your report card from school.

W: Hi, boys and girls.

P: I said, here is your report card from school.

W: Hi, boys and girls.

P: Pay attention. Are you trying to make a fool of me?

W: Too late.

P: Just look at this report. Spelling, zero. Arithmetic, zero. Reading, zero.

W: I'm consistent, eh?

P: You're at the foot of your class. Why don't you try to get to the head of the class?

W: Why? They teach the same things at both ends.

P: Your teacher said you spelled needle N-E-I-D-L-E.

W: That's right

P: That's wrong. There is no "I" in needle.

W: Then how you going to thread it?

P: Let's try Arithmetic. If you had a quarter—

W: I ain't got a quarter.

P: Just imagine you had a quarter.

W: I ain't got that much imagination.

P: If you had a quarter, and loaned me fifteen cents, what would you have left?

W: A quarter.

P: You don't get my meaning.

W: You don't get my fifteen cents.

P: If you had ten dollars in this pants pocket and five dollars in this pants pocket, what would you have?

W: Somebody else's pants.

P: Here's you last chance. If I gave you a nickel on Sunday—

W: You wouldn't do it.

P: Oh, yes I would. I give you a nickel on Sunday and every day of the week I give you a nickel, how many nickels would you have at the end of the week?

W: Nine nickels.

P: That's impossible. There are only seven days in a week.

W: But I already have two nickels.

P: Why don't you study. Don't you want to grow up to be a gentleman and a scholar?

W: No, I want to be like you.

P: What a future. Let's go to the woodshed.

A Visit With Uncle Eddie

Windy: That's me, Windy Higgins.

Paul: Hi everybody. This is Paul Stadelman.

W: What, no silly title today?

P: Not today. We don't have time. Uncle Eddie will be here in a minute.

W: So what?

P: Aren't you excited that at last Uncle Eddie will be on your show?

W: Uncle Eddie is just a joke.

P: No, he is real. He is not a myth.

W: He is not a what?

P: A myth. You know what a myth is.

W: Sure I do. A lady moth.

P: Your Uncle Eddie is really Eddie Fritz, the producer of our show, and I want all of our friends to meet him now. Come out of the woodshed, Eddie. (Eddie comes out, smiles and bows.)

W: (Slowly, to camera.) Well, whatta you know.

Eddie: What do you know, Windy?

W: Oh, no I asked you first.

P: Come on, shake hands with Uncle Eddie.

W: Are his hands clean?

P: That isn't nice.

W: No, it's sanitary.

W: (Shaking hands with Eddie). Don't you feel silly shaking hands with a dummy?

E: I certainly do.

W: So do I.

P: You promised you would be nice to Eddie. Say something nice to him.

W: He's ugly.

P: That's not nice.

W: It's true (Eddie looks mournful).

P: You've hurt Eddie's feelings.

W: Where there's no sense, there's no feelings.

P: Now you apologize to Uncle Eddie.

W: How do I do that?

P: You said he was ugly. Tell him you're sorry.

W: Uncle Eddie, I'm sorry you're so ugly.

E: (Angry.) I've had enough of this, you splinter. Do you see this? (Doubles up fist under Windy's nose).

W: Dirty, isn't it? (Eddie splutters, mumbles and puts his hand into his pocket).

P: Now you have Uncle Eddie mad enough to fight, and he is bigger than you.

W: Shucks, I can lick him with one hand tied.

E: I'd like to see you do it.

P: So would I. How can you lick him with one hand tied?

W: You tie his hand and I'll show you.

P: Into the woodshed for you!

Halloween

(Paul has on false nose and glasses.)

Windy: That's me, Windy Higgins.

Paul: Hi, everybody, and a happy Halloween to all.

W: What's Halloween?

P: You ask the silliest questions.

W: And I get the silliest answers.

P: Halloween is a time for parties, ducking for apples, and wearing false faces to scare people.

W: Why don't you do that?

P: Do what?

W: Wear a false face.

P: Don't you notice anything about me?

W: New necktie?

P: No.

W: Haircut?

P: No. (Paul takes off nose.)

W: (Windy looks at Paul's face, then looks at Paul.) Take it off!

P: I did take it off. This is my real nose.

W: I like the other one better.

P: Say, I'm tired of your insults. And I'm jealous too.

W: No wonder, I'm cuter.

P: It isn't that. You get all the laughs. I want some funny lines.

W: With that face, you don't need funny lines.

P: Well, let's try one. You help me.

W: All right, go ahead.

P: Windy, did you see the morning paper?

W: No, what's in it?

P: My lunch. Ha, ha.

W: Quiet in here, isn't it?

P: Let's just try one more.

W: This is the last.

P: All right, this is the last. Windy, did you see the big race?

W: No.

P: You are supposed to say "what race?"

W: I don't care.

P: I thought you were going to help.

W: All right, do it again.

P: Windy, did you see the big race?

W: What race?

P: The human race. Ha, ha, ha.
W: What are you laughing at? You're not in it!

You Drive Me Crazy

Paul: Never again will I take you driving in my car!
Windy: Why not?
P: You looked at my car like it was the first car you ever saw.
W: Your car looks like the first car I ever saw.
P: You wouldn't think it was a second hand car, would you?
W: No, it looks like you made it yourself.
P: My car is called a Mercury.
W: You should call it "snake." It always rattles before it strikes.
P: What would you do if you were driving and the brakes failed. What would you do?
W: I'd try to hit something cheap.
P: If I had the money, I would have the car overhauled, but it would take lots of money.
W: Uncle Eddie had his car overhauled for only $50.
P: How was that?
W: He was going 80 and a cop overhauled him. Cost him $50.
P: How did you like that ride in my car last week?
W: That was fun. I'm going to get a car of my own.
P: That's foolish Why do you want to get a car?
W: I just found a parking place.
P: Where?
W: On State Street, right in front of the studio.
P: It's against the law to park there.
W: Oh, no, didn't you see the sign?
P: What did the sign say?
W: It didn't say anything. You have to read it.
P: Smarty, what was on the sign?
W: Fine for parking here."
P: Had any punctures yet?
W: Just one.
P: Where was that?
W: In the tire. Where do you think?

P: I meant, where were you when you got it?
W: At a fork in the road, where else?
P: You must have been in the country.
W: Yeah, I guess so. I wasn't hitting so many people.
P: I'm never going to ride with you again.
W: Why not.
P: You got a ticket for running a stop sign; couldn't you read?
W: Sure, but I couldn't stop.
P: You were driving too fast.
W: I had to. The breaks were no good and I wanted to rush
   home before I had an accident.
P: And then you ran over that poor old man.
W: You told me to.
P: I did not. I said"Give him the right of way."
W: Oh, I thought you said "Get him right away."
P: To the woodshed!

NOVELTY DIALOGUES

The Talking Dog
(This is a simple routine using a typical balloon dog.)
You: This is my pet dog Ralph. Say "Hi" Ralph.
Ralph: Ruff! Ruff!
Y: Now Ralph here isn't your every day ordinary dog—he's a
   BALLOON dog. But what is even more amazing is that
   Ralph can talk. That's right, he can talk just like you or I . . .
   I can see by the looks on your faces you don't believe me . . .
   I'll prove it to you, I'll ask Ralph some questions and he'll
   answer back in plain English. You ready Ralph?
R: Ruff! Ruff!
Y: To start off, tell us your name. What's your name—say it so
   everyone can hear.
R: Ralph! Ralph! (Spoken in a barking tone.)
Y: That's right, it's Ralph. Very good . . . . (Looking at the
   audience.) I told you he could do it. But that's not all. Here's

another question. What grows on the outside of trees?

R: Bark! Bark! (Spoken as if barking.)

Y: You're right again. Let's see if you can answer another question. What covers a house?

R: Roof! Roof!

Y: Of course, the roof covers a house. (Looking at audience.) See I told you he could talk. (Looking back at the dog.) You're doing so well let me ask you a hard question this time. What is another word for Dad?

R: (Silence.)

Y: Come on I know you can say it. What is another name for Dad?

R: Err. (Said in a quiet muffled tone.)

Y: What was that? You have to speak louder so everyone can hear.

R: Err. (Again said quietly.)

Y: (Lean your head next to Ralph's.) Speak up, louder, we can't hear you. What's another name for Dad?

R: POP! (Balloon is punctured so it explodes in your ear.)

Y: (As the balloon pops, jump back in surprise and scram grabbing your ears.) OOOOH! . . . That's right, it's "POP." Talking is very hard on dogs, especially balloon dogs, and it always takes a lot out of Ralph as you can see. (The long wormy looking deflated balloon is held up for everyone to see.) . . . Now I would like to introduce you to my talking worm — Ralph . . .

Old MacDonald's Funny Farm

This routine and the following three — Christmas Turkey, Gator on Vacation, and The Magic Drawing Board — use puppets and props manufactured by Axtell Expressions. The dialogues which accompany each routine were written by Steve Axtell and are used with his permission.

You: (Watching the old story teller puppet chewing and moving his face will start your routine with lots of laughs.) Hello sir, my name is _____, what is your name? (He cannot hear too well so you repeat and startle him.)

Old McDonald: Howdy, I'm Old MacDonald.

Y: (Look surprised to your audience) Oh come now, surely your kidding!

O: I'm not kidding and I'm not Shirley. I'm Old MacDonald.

Y: You're the Old MacDonald from the song Old MacDonald Had a Farm?

O: (Slowly and straining he sings.) E-I-E-I-O! (He begins coughing from straining his voice.)

Y: (Patting his back.) Are you all right?

O: (Recovering.) Yeah, I'm just old.

Y: How old are you?

O: (Annoyed, his face pulls tightly together in response to your question then slowly releases.) My age is MY business!

Y: (To audience.) I bet he's been in business a long time!

O: Look sonny, I'll tell the jokes!

Y: How can you tell when you're old?

O: There's three ways to tell if you're getting old. One, a loss of memory, the second . . . (Pull his eyebrows down slowly as if he forgot.) . . . I forget.

Y: They say you start to lose your hearing as you get older, is that true?

O: What? I'm just kidding, (laughs at his own joke). I've got the body of a twenty year old.

Y: (Look at his body, then at the audience.) How's your eyesight?

O: My vision is 20/20 . . . (He looks at you.) Hmm! So how long have YOU been wearing glasses? (This joke only works if you're not wearing glasses.)

Y: I'm not! (Bring the puppet's head in close, squinting to see your face, then when he realizes his mistake he goes into his face scrunch.) How's your sense of smell?

O: Funny you should mention that! (He begins smelling you, moving his nose up and down and sniffing.)

Y: (Backing away.) What are you doing?

O: Did you put on your deodorant this morning?
Y: Yes! I used Ban Roll-On.
O: Well, it smells like it rolled off!
Y: Old MacDonald, it isn't me . . . I wasn't going to mention it, but you smell like the barnyard.
O: Well I just came from feeding the pigs.
Y: How long have you been raising pigs?
O: Forty-eight years.
Y: Seems like they'd be grown up by now.
O: I said I'll tell the jokes, sonny!
Y: Do you have any other animals?
O: Yeah, I got a whole flock of cows.
Y: Not flock, herd.
O: Heard what?
Y: Herd of cows.
O: Well sure I've heard of cows . . . I said I got a whole flock of them!
Y: So, do you only have livestock?
O: Well no, some have died.
Y: Have you tried raising crops?
O: Yeah, but no luck. I planted acres and acres of straw, and I didn't get one single strawberry.
Y: You don't get strawberries from straw.
O: Oh. How do you get them?
Y: I don't know, you get a strawberry plant and you put it in the ground and water it, then you put fertilizer on it and—
O: (Shocked.) You put fertilizer on strawberries?
Y: Well sure . . . what do you put on them?
O: Cream and sugar.
Y: You must put in a long day.
O: I work 25 hours a day.
Y: How could you? There are only 24 hours in a day.
O: I get up an hour early.
Y: Old MacDonald, would you sing the song that made you famous?

O: I get short of breath so why don't you sing with me.

Y: You mean sing together?

O: No, you're not THAT good. I'll sing the first line and you sing the next and so on. (Singing.) Old MacDonald had a farm . . .

Y: G-I-G-I-Joe. (Puppet's face is appearing angry and slowly turns toward you so you begin singing to avoid his comments.) Old MacDonald had a farm . . .

O: E-I-E-I-O.

Y: Excuse me, but for years I've wondered what does E-I-E-I-O mean? There must be some real significance like a code or message; it's always made me curious and now, finally I can ask the one who knows. (Dramatically.) Old MacDonald, what does E-I-E-I-O mean?

O: Nothing. I was typing the song out on the typewriter, sneezed and my fingers hit the wrong keys.

Y: WHAT? E-I-E-I-O is a typographical error? Why did you leave it in the song?

O: I lost the White-Out. I'm just lucky it was a good sneeze.

Y: A good sneeze? What do you mean?

O: Well just imagine . . . Old MacDonald had a farm, II-I-Q-L-R.

Y: I see what you mean . . . let's just sing the song . . . Old MacDonald had a farm . . .

O: E-I-E-I-O.

Y: And on his farm he had a duck . . .

O: No, I didn't. Just pigs and cows.

Y: (Annoyed.) And on his farm he had a pig.

O: E-I-E-I-O.

Y: With a—

O: Oink, oink—

Y: Here, and a—

O: Oink, oink—

Y: There, here a—

O: Oink—

Y: There a—

O: Oink—

Y: Everywhere a—
O: (Out of breath.) Good grief this pig talks a lot!
Y: Old MacDonald had a farm—
O: (Big finish.) E-I . . . (Takes a deep breath and cough.) E-I
   . . . (Deep breath again, cough and then finish as if it hurts.)
   Ohhhh . . .
Y: Old MacDonald your voice is all it's cracked up to be. Thanks
   for coming today. (He continues to cough as you take a bow.)

Christmas Turkey
You: Ladies and gentlemen, may I present to you someone who is
   a real "turkey!" So . . . I see you made it through Thanks
   giving. What were YOU thankful for?
Turkey: That I made it through Thanksgiving!
Y: Do you know what follows Thanksgiving?
T: Indigestion!
Y: No . . . Christmas. Didn't your parents ever tell you about
   Christmas? (Stare at each other.) No, I guess not. (Put the
   Santa hat on the turkey's head.)
T: What are you doing?
Y: I'm dressing you up. Everyone likes a "dressed turkey" for
   Christmas too.
T: How do I look?
Y: Like a turkey. You look very nice, the reason I brought you
   out here and dressed you up is that these nice people invited
   us to a "roast" in your honor.
T: Get me out of here! (Make the bird attempt to leap from your
   arms and pretend to catch him.)
Y: Calm down. I'm just kidding. Say, can you sing?
T: I can sing, dance, play the piano, AND . . . I do windows!
Y: Well then, sing a Christmas song for us—sing "Jingle Bells."
T: O.K., but how I'm not sure of all the words, can you help
   me?
Y: Sure, I'll help you out with the words, just sing the chorus.
T: (Warming up.) Mee mee mee la la la (pause). How does it
   start?

Y: Jingle bells.
T: Oh yeah. Jingle bells . . .
Y: Again!
T: Jingle bells, jingle bells . . . jingle all the way—
Y: Oh what fun—
T: (Turkey looks at you.) I'm glad you're enjoying yourself!
Y: Those are the next words.
T: Oh. Oh what fun it is to ride in a . . .
Y: Well, what's fun to ride in?
T: A roller coaster!
Y: That's true, but the song say's 'a one horse open sleigh.'
T: What? . . . If you say so. Oh what fun it is to ride in a one
   horse open sleigh—
Y: Hey!
T: (The turkey looks at you.) What?
Y: Hey!
T: What do you want?
Y: That's next! "Hey" is next.
T: Is that so the one horse will have something to eat?
Y: No, "hey" is just an expression to show you're having a good
   time.
T: But I'm not!
Y: Just sing it.
T: Oh what fun it is to ride in a one horse open sleigh . . . hey!
Y: Thank you.
T: You're welcome.
Y: Now sing the whole chorus.
T: Jingle bells, jingle bells, jingle . . . that's a lot of jingling. . .
   all the way . . . oh what fun it is to ride in a one (end the
   song by slowing down and rising your pitch) horse . . . o . . .
   pen. . . roller coaster!!

Gator On Vacation
You: (To audience.) Hello, my name is _____ , what's
   yours?

Gator: You can call me Al.

Y: Where are you from Al?

G: Miami, Florida. (Or Louisiana if you're in Florida.)

Y: Nice that you could be with us, does it get hot in Florida?

G: Yeah boy! I gotta drink lots of "Gatorade" to stay cool.

Y: How does an alligator get here from Florida? Did you swim?

G: (Sarcastically.) Did you swim? . . . No, I flew.

Y: Come on, Al. Alligators can't fly.

G: Tell American Airlines that.

Y: You came on a plane?

G: No, I came IN a plane. They thought I was a suitcase.

Y: (Look at Al's body then hold his tail up to your waist.) I can tell how they would think that, your tail would make a great belt too.

G: (Angry.) Watch it Buddy.

Y: (Put the tail down slowly) S-s-sorry Al. You came on a plane . . . I would have been afraid of a terrorist.

G: I met a terrorist at the airport. He thought I was a suitcase, and tried to put a bomb in me. Man was he surprised!

Y: Did you chew him up?

G: No, but I sure took a bite out of crime!

Y: (Looking at his jaws.) Wow, you really do have powerful jaws — like a vise!

G: Yeah, they call me the "Miami Vice."

Y: My what big teeth you have. Do you brush your teeth?

G: Yes, and I dental floss too . . . with snakes!

Y: Do you go to the dentist?

G: I try, but every time I go they always say the same thing. . . "open wide." (The gator's mouth opens toward you and you jump back scared.) I lose more dentists that way.

Y: Maybe you should go to a veterinarian.

G: A Who?

Y: An animal doctor.

G: They're letting animals be doctors now?

Y: No, a veterinarian takes care of animals.

G: Oh, like the one that kept me in that little hot thing, till I hatched?

Y: You were hatched in an incubator?

G: No, a crock pot!

Y: Well Al, it's been great talking to you. (Look out at the audience and wink as if you're clever.) See you later alligator. (Laugh at your joke, while gator becomes angry and slowly turns his head toward you.)

G: Cute.

Y: After a while crocodile. (Laugh again at your joke.)

G: You better watch it bud, or you'll lose all your money.

Y: (Confused.) How will I lose all my money?

G: Your alligator wallet is a good friend of mine.

Y: You two know each other?

Distant voice of wallet: That's right!

Y: (Look scared to audience, then to gator, then to wallet) No way.

G: Sic him Wally!

Y: OUCH! (Jump as if bitten from behind.)

G: Told you.

Y: OK, sorry Al . . . I'll just put you back in your leather case . . . or are you friends with it too?

G: Yes. He's my bodyguard!

The Magic Drawing Board
(Use this dialogue after the drawing comes to life.)

A: Are you alive?

M: Write-on!

A: What is your name?

M: Art (or Mark).

A: You look like a "square." Do you have a girl friend?

M: Yes, her name is Nancy "Drew."

A: Is she cute?

M: She's as pretty as a "picture."

A: Do you have a family?

M: I can't hear you very well, my ears are too small.

A: I'll take care of that for you. (Artist erases ears and draws bigger ones.) There. Now can you hear me?

M: You don't have to yell!

A: Hey, that's where I draw the line.

M: Must be nice all I can draw is flies.

A: Why? Do you smell?

M: Not with a magic marker nose I can't smell.

A: OK. I'm going to have to "draw" this to a conclusion . . besides, Art, you look "bored." (Tap your knuckles on the board.)

M: Yeah this was a rotten sketch anyway.

A: Say good-bye, Art. (Start erasing him from bottom up.)

M: (Yelling.) I've been "framed!" Hey don't do that I'll be good. I'm really wiped out. Hey, "picture" this, we could have a " "board" meeting . . . mmmm-mmm-mmm- mmmm. (The mouth is erased followed by the rest of the face.)

A: (The board is blank and the artist looks at the marker.) I guess that's why they call these "Magic Markers."

APPENDIX

ADVANCED VENTRILOQUISM

If you have followed me thus far, I am sure you will have a good understanding of ventriloquism, and I hope you will have a desire to put into practice the principles learned. Just remember when you started your first driving lesson: you had to let up on the accelerator, depress the clutch, shift to the right gear, release the clutch, depress the accelerator, and at the same time steer the car and watch the traffic. It seemed difficult at first, but after some practice you now go through all this without any conscious effort on your part, and driving is a pleasure. Your ventriloquism will be just as easy in a short while. All the things you have learned will blend together.

In this book I have presented ventriloquism in a simple easy-to-learn manner and described how to use it with a variety of puppets. I've purposely deleted many of the finer points of ventriloquism so as not to confuse or discourage you. With the knowledge I've given in this book you have all the groundwork necessary to become a good ventriloquist.

As in any area of knowledge there is always more that can be learned. If you would like to improve your techniques for talking and manipulating a vent figure, I would highly recommend that you take Maher Studios Home Study Ventriloquism Course. Maher Studios has been serving ventriloquists and puppeteers for over 60 years. Their home study course covers everything from the basics to advanced techniques, and even includes information on how to secure jobs as a ventriloquist. The course consists of 30 lessons with cassette tapes, instruction booklets, practice dialogues, and a ventril-o-aid device to help control lip movement. All students are given lifetime permission to write or call the Maher office for any help or information they may need to further their development with ventriloquism.

Many of the professional ventriloquists working today are graduates of Maher's course. To find out more about this course, contact Maher Studios.

RESOURCES

Many magic shops carry instruction books, tapes, dialogues, puppets, ventriloquial figures, puppet patterns and accessories. If you can't find a source in your area for these items you can contact the sources below.

Axtell Expressions
2889 Bunsen Ave H
Ventura, CA 93003 USA
www.axtell.com

Davenports
7 Adelaides Street
London WC2N 4HZ, UK
www.davenportsmagic.co.uk

GFE Magic and Ventriloquism
118 Wellington Dr
Hull, GA 30646
www.magicandventriloquism.com

Mastercraft Puppets
4110 SE Hawthorne Blvd. #426
Portland, OR 97214
www.mastercraftpuppets.com

Maher Studios
Box 420
Littleton, CO 80160 USA
www.maherstudios.com

One Way Street, Inc.
11999 E Caley Ave
Englewood, CO 80111 USA
www.onewaystreet.com

Puppets & More
1025 E. Yoke Street
Indianapolis, IN 46203 USA

The Puppetry Store
302 W Latham St
Phoenix AZ 85003 USA

Selberg Studios
1034 Betts Rd
Leonard, MI 48367 USA
www.selbergstudios.com

Show-Biz Services
1735 East 26th Street
Brooklyn, NY 11229 USA

Vent Haven Museum
33 West Maple
Fort Mitchell, KY 41011 USA
www.venthaven.com

INDEX